PENGUINS
A WORLDWIDE GUIDE

Rémy Marion

Illustrations by
Sylviane Maigret-Mondry

Sterling Publishing Co., Inc.
New York

Library of Congress Cataloging-in-Publication Data Available

Acknowledgements and photocredits may be found on page 154.

10 9 8 7 6 5 4 3 2 1

Published by Sterling Publishing Company, Inc.
387 Park Avenue South, New York, N.Y. 10016
Originally published in France under the title *Guide des Manchots* by Rémy Martin
and © 1995 by Delachaux et Niestlé S.A., Lausanne (Switzerland)
English translation © 1999 by Sterling Publishing Company, Inc.
Distributed in Canada by Sterling Publishing
℅ Canadian Manda Group, One Atlantic Avenue, Suite 105
Toronto, Ontario, Canada M6K 3E7
Distributed in Great Britain and Europe by Cassell PLC
Wellington House, 125 Strand, London WC2R 0BB, England
Distributed in Australia by Capricorn Link (Australia) Pty Ltd.
P.O. Box 6651, Baulkham Hills, Business Centre, NSW 2153, Australia
Printed in Hong Kong

Sterling ISBN 0-8069-4232-0

CONTENTS

A rockhopper calling out after returning from the sea, Falkland Islands

Procession of emperor penguins crossing Cape Crozier, Antárctica

PREFACE

Everyone sees penguins in a different way. But the truth is that they are animals that have adapted so well to their harsh environment that we tend to forget that they are first and foremost birds.

Exceptional divers, austral ocean adventurers, and pack-ice enthusiasts, penguins have evolved amazing survival strategies.

They nest on a few favorable sites on the Antarctic coast, subantarctic islands, and southern shores of the major continents. Their land-nesting habits have enabled people to study them around the world.

However, most of their life is spent at sea beyond the pack ice, chasing the squid, fish, and krill, in order to ensure the propagation of the species.

We must preserve these food sources if we want to continue to see emperor penguins trudging across the sea ice, season after season, and to behold the steep and treacherous slopes of the most inhospitable islands and peninsulas filled miraculously within days with a loud and odorous multitude.

We have been visiting penguin colonies for more than 20 years, and it is the sheer numbers, density, and activity that have left the most lasting impressions.

Thousands, sometimes hundreds of thousands, of penguins may be gathered in a small area, squawking, beating their flippers, and engaging in displays. We might spot a skua, resembling a big, brown sea gull, snatching a penguin egg or stealing food out of a chick's bill, or see a sea leopard, feared predator, slowly patrolling. These are powerful images that we hope will never become a rarity or disappear altogether.

Learning about penguins, getting to know them better, and helping others to know them better may prevent us from ever treating these incredible birds negligently. This book is a good step in the right direction.

Jérôme and Sally Poncet
Yacht Damien II at Grytviken, South Georgia

INTRODUCTION

The first part of this book is an overview of the origins and evolution of *Spheniscidae* (the family of penguins) and of their biology. The second part describes the distinctive characteristics of the 17 species that contribute to the richness of this unique family. The last part recounts the interactions between penguins and people. And the appendix includes sections on the environment and the feeding habits of *Spheniscidae*.

The distribution maps for these Antarctic and subantarctic species are based on Woelher's works from 1993, and show the range of the different species' colonies and foraging grounds. Vagrant records are not shown. Distribution zones are colored in red, land in white, and seas in blue.

Colored graphs will help you visualize the composition of the diet of the various species and the amount of each type of prey consumed within a given site; dark blue stands for crustaceans, red for fish, and purple for cephalopods.

The black-and-white plates at the end of the book depict penguins' most common prey. These represent about 20 percent of all known prey.

This guide is a synthesis of the latest data concerning the *Spheniscidae* family (as of 1994). Research in penguin biology and ethology is advancing rapidly due to the efforts of many people and new methods of investigation. Consequently, new data might have been published since this manuscript was copyrighted.

In light of the many letters and phone calls I have received, I believe this book will benefit researchers, students, journalists, and naturalists, and interest all animal lovers.

Penguins have managed to adapt to the Earth's most extreme weather conditions thanks to the diversification of the family, their wide distribution range across all southern latitudes, and 50 million years of evolution. Comparing penguins to humans, and failing to recognize the unique characteristics of both species, is to doom penguins to extinction. Try to imagine the sea populated only with sardines, the sky only with gulls, and the land only with humans. . . .

Rémy Marion

GENERALITIES
ORIGINS AND EVOLUTION

Explorers long described penguins as flightless "sub-birds"—half-fish, half-birds.

In the early 19th century, Dumont d'Urville, an Antarctic explorer, wrote: "This fish-bird, which we already observed on Tristan da Cunha Island, is built to swim rather than fly. Instead of wings, it has two flattened flippers, and its body is covered with a tight felt resembling silk more than feathers. Its little paddles seem to be covered in scales."

The study of the origins of this family shows that the level of evolution of present-day *Spheniscidae* is one of the most specialized and complex.

These apterous (wingless) birds don't descend from *Ratitae* (the division of birds that are unable to fly), as we might expect, but from birds most adept at flying: *Procellariiformes*. This group of primitive birds is comprised of species remarkably adapted to flight: albatrosses, shearwaters, and petrels. Birds of the high seas, they are found in the skies over all the oceans of the world.

Fossil studies suggest a cousinship between today's petrels and penguins. Penguins, like birds that are volant (capable of flying), have a keeled breastbone that supports the pectoral muscles required for flying, which sets them apart from kiwis, emus, and other *Ratitae*.

As with volant birds, the penguin possesses a cerebellum with structures specific to tridimensional movement. The presence of horny plates on the bill of the little penguin *(Eudyptula minor)*—considered the most primitive species—is also reminiscent of that of petrels and albatrosses. *Procellariiformes* and penguins share nocturnal and ground-nesting habits, as well.

The physiology of penguins evolved under the pressures of their marine environment. This evolution converged remarkably with that of other animal species, such as seals and dolphins.

Even though penguins don't fly in the air, it could be said that they fly underwater, because their subaquatic movements seem so aerial. This is made possible by their having a powerful pectoral belt supported by a strong breastbone. Their dorsal muscles are more developed than those of volant birds and are largely responsible for their efficient underwater flight.

A pair of albatross, a cousin of the penguin

The evolution of their wings is the most notable part of their long adaptation. Water resistance is 20 times greater than that of air. Their fragile wings had to adapt themselves into rigid paddles to overcome their resistance to efficient underwater movement. Their bones flattened and became stronger and more hydrodynamic. Out of all the original joints, only the shoulders remained mobile. The biceps, no longer used, disappeared. Their ability to fold their flippers became greatly restricted. At the same time, their tendinous system became modified to rigidify their flippers until they could no longer flex or extend. Their feet became more hydrodynamic, and were set toward the rear of the body, like palmipeds (web-footed birds). However, penguins were still supported by a strongly developed pelvic belt, which enabled them to move about on land and take big leaps.

Tarsometatarsus from three penguin species, from left to right: king, gentoo, and rockhopper

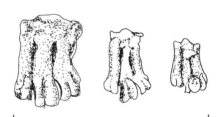

10 cm (3.9 inches)

Feet of the rockhopper penguin

The evolution of the penguin's tarsometatarsus (in birds, the large bone in the lower part of the leg) is so notable that it helps differentiate penguins from other birds and is essential in identifying fossils.

The size of the tarsometatarsus is directly proportional to the size of the penguin. It is particularly large in *Aptenodytes* (the penguin genus comprising the king and the emperor) and supports three powerful claws.

It can be said that their bone structure became denser in order to increase rigidity and make submersion easier.

Their long and light feathers became short and rigid to increase thermal insulation and facilitate water penetration. The polar species were faced with harsh climatic conditions—extreme for the emperor penguin—that led to several physiological changes and unique behavioral adaptations.

It becomes quite obvious that penguins are far from being "sub-birds" but rather are the product of a long and elaborate evolution.

The first signs of the evolution of modern penguins' ancestors appeared about 50 million years ago, between the late Paleocene and early Eocene epochs.

Protopetrels that lived around 45° south latitude were not subjected to land predators, so they lost their ability to fly. Like today's petrels, they were already good swimmers, and when they stopped flying they used their wings to propel themselves underwater.

The Southern Hemisphere was much different then. Gondwana had just broken up into scattered continents, but Australia, New Zealand, and Antarctica were still close to one another. South America was not connected to North America; instead, it was tied to the Antarctic Peninsula through a string of islands that now form the Scotia Arc. Whales and other *Pinnipedia* did not yet exist. They appeared in the seas south of the equator during the mid-Oligocene and early Miocene epochs.

11

Comparative History of Penguins, *Alcidae*, and Marine Mammals

(According to Fordyce R. E. and Jones C. M., 1990)

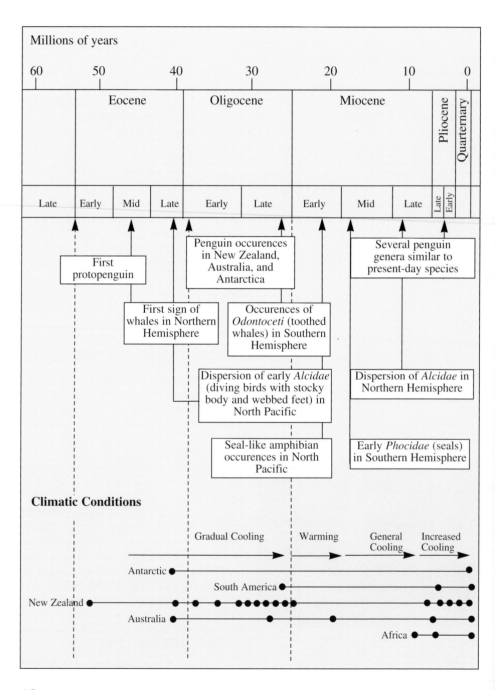

Latitudinal Dispersion and Evolutionary History of Penguin Species

(According to Toll, 1978; Schreiweiss, 1982)

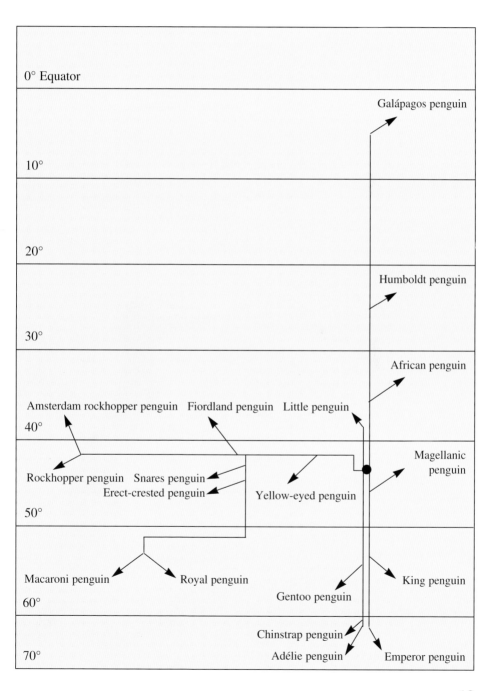

The distribution of *Spheniscidae* followed the placement of currents in the austral ocean (see "Introduction to Antarctic Oceanography" in the appendix).

Current fossil discoveries give no indication of the evolution of these protopenguins between the mid-Oligocene and late Eocene epochs. The family seems to have started dispersing 38 million years ago: Seymour Island in Antarctica was already host to 14 species; Australia was home to *Anthropornis nordenskjoeldi,* a penguin the size of a human that stood 5 feet (1.50 m) tall; and New Zealand also had developed an important penguin population with 14 documented species.

It was not until the late Miocene epoch (10 million years ago) that penguins started occupying their present-day distribution zone. The species, now extinct, are thought to have resembled today's penguins.

Paleontologists are faced with a difficult task, because most fossils are broken into many pieces. However, they are able to estimate the size and the state of evolution of the species through a comparative study of the resistant and calcified humerus and tarsometatarsus.

The paleontological data is supported by biochemical analyses that confirm the relationship between penguins and the super-family of *Procellariidae,* comprising divers, albatrosses, petrels, and frigate birds.

Evolution of the Species

The distribution and speciation of penguins were determined by two factors: the Southern Hemisphere's hydrographic conditions and the presence of land. Each species inhabits regions fed by cold water currents (less than 68° F, or 20° C) coming directly from the Antarctic Circumpolar Current or its ramifications. The richness of nutrients brought by these currents varies according to the season. Penguins (except the Galápagos) have adapted their annual cycles to the seasons in order to have the most resources available to feed their chicks.

Parallels and isothermic lines overlap and help define latitudinal distribution, with New Zealand as base point at 45° south latitude. The six *Eudyptes* species are distributed roughly from 40° to 60° latitude between the Antarctic and Subtropical Convergences, where temperatures remain stable at between 43° and 68° F, or 6° and 20° C. They have developed different morphological characteristics (crests and flippers) and vocal traits, because they are isolated from one another. The *Spheniscus* species, on the other hand, adapted to relatively warm climates. Continental up-wellings (see "Introduction to Austral Oceanography" in the appendix) enabled them to disperse northward, up to the equator.

Comparison to Other Birds

Penguins resemble auks and other *Alcidae,* so much so that people mistake them for one another. Their adaptive con-

A great auk, an apterous Alcidae, *which became extinct in the early 19th century (drawing based on a stuffed specimen)*

vergence has caused much confusion. Auks are marine birds with the same counter-shaded camouflage plumage as penguins': white on the underparts to avoid detection by underwater predators when they are at the surface of the water, and black on the back to disappear in the depths of the ocean. *Alcidae,* like penguins, propel themselves underwater with their wings. The wings of *Alcidae* have not yet evolved into flippers, because they are still used for aerial flight, however heavy and clumsy they may be. Auks once had an apterous cousin: the great auk (*Alca impennis*). It was the size of a penguin and lived on islands in the Northern Hemisphere. The last one died in 1844.

Little auks, Alcidae *family, from the polar regions, Svalbard*

Wingless species exist in every bird family: the weka (*Galliralus australis*) in the *Rallidae* family, the steamer duck (*Tachyeres brachydactyla*) in the *Anatidae* family, the flightless cormorant (*Nannopterum harrisi*) in the *Pele-*

canidae family, and the great auk (*Alca impennis*) in the *Alcidae* family.

None of these birds has developed its forelimbs as penguins have, even though they have lost their ability to fly because of the lack of land predators. Their wings, which are now useless, hang

Flightless steamer ducks from the Falklands escaping to sea

15

alongside their body or disappear under their thick belly feathers. The steamer duck, however, uses its wings like paddle-wheels to quickly escape when necessary.

BIOLOGY

Hearing and Vocal Communication

Penguins have good hearing. Their auditory acuity, like humans', ranges from 30 to 12,500 Hz.

Penguins breed in very dense colonies of up to several thousand birds. Lost in the multitude and clothed in identical plumage, they were forced to develop a reliable way of recognizing their mate and chicks during the breeding season, and vocalizations became the key.

Each bird has its own sound ID. They recognize each other through variations in the amplitude and length of each calling sequence, because they are capable of a very fine resolution (around 15 ms). Penguin sonograms can be compared to our own fingerprints or bar codes. Each species is unique in that it possesses a common vocal pattern, but the structure of the calls varies between the male and the female.

Smell

Smell doesn't play an important role in penguins' relationships with one another or their environment. Their cerebral lobe that controls olfaction is of average size.

Vision

Penguins are amphibious animals, par excellence. They live off the sea and generally use their sight to locate and capture prey. Their eyes are wide open underwater. The cornea is protected by a nictitating membrane with vertical motion that cleans it constantly.

Penguins' visual capabilities have been studied extensively. However, research conducted on different species has led to differing conclusions, so there is no one theory that can be applied to all *Spheniscidae*.

Research conducted by Sivak and Millodot on four species (king, rockhopper, gentoo, and Cape) demonstrates that they are slightly nearsighted in the air and farsighted underwater (between 8

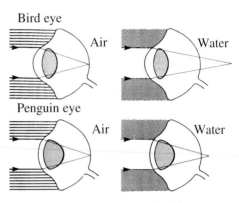

Penguin vision, according to Sivak, 1980

and 13 diopters compared to 40 diopters for humans).

The blurry underwater vision of humans is due to the difference in the refractive index between the water and the cornea. Light is focused behind the retina. This phenomenon can be altered through the adaptation of the cornea.

Measurements show that the degree of curvature of the cornea is far greater in penguins than in species evolving only on land or in the sea. The cornea is flat, so the change in visual resolution between air and water is much less. For instance, seals, which are nearsighted on land, contract their pupils (focusing lens) into a vertical slit, reducing the active area of the cornea and consequently the variations in refraction that result from a curved cornea.

According to Sivak and Millodot, underwater farsightedness is not a hindrance because of the spectral characteristics of the water.

The works of Martin and Young on the Humboldt penguin (*Spheniscus humboldti*) offer a different analysis. Humboldts appear to be nearsighted on land (28 diopters), but they have normal underwater vision.

Their photoreceptors show a high sensitivity to colors underwater, particularly the blue or blue-green end of the spectrum with wavelengths close to 500 nm. The penguin's eyes become inefficient beyond 550 nm toward the red end of the spectrum, because they don't have red-sensitive cells.

However, penguins have good low-light vision, which enables them to forage at great depths. Their retina is similar to that of nocturnal birds, compensating efficiently for the lack of light by a quick dilation of the pupil.

The *Spheniscus* species doesn't have short-range stereoscopic vision. This is obvious when standing close to an African or a magellanic penguin: first it looks with the right eye and then the left, while nodding its head. This monocular vision can be explained by the lateral position of the eyes due to the presence of a thick bill that blocks short-range vision, not allowing the bird to overlap two identical images. However, penguins' stereoscopic field of view underwater is very expansive vertically (125°), and it allows them to see prey swimming above them. Thus, they hunt by swimming under fish shoals that are no longer invisible due to the surface light reflecting on their underparts.

The Social Role of Color

Yellow seems to be an important color in penguins' social and sexual relationships. *Eudyptes* penguins, with their discolored yellow crests, have trouble attracting a mate. Immature birds have yet to grow their yellow plumes, which appear when they reach adulthood.

The little penguin (*Eudyptula minor*), a nocturnal species, has no distinctive color markings.

Adaptation to Diving

Penguins feed exclusively on small marine animals—fish, cephalopods, and crustaceans—and they must dive to catch their prey.

Their pulmonary respiratory system had to adapt considerably to this subaquatic life.

This homeothermic (warm-blooded), amphibious animal has to:

1. Reach depths where the most sought-after prey are found
2. Conserve body temperature

A Galápagos penguin foraging (drawing above and photo on pages 18–19)

3. Withstand increased underwater pressure

This requires oxygen that cannot be provided through the lungs while diving. Penguins must therefore store a certain amount of oxygen and manage this reserve efficiently.

Vertebrates have three options for storing vital oxygen:
1. In lung alveoli
2. In myoglobin (protein in muscle tissue)
3. In hemoglobin (protein in the blood)

It is interesting to compare the ratios of

	Lungs	Muscles	Blood
Adélie penguin	29%	33%	38%
Weddell seal	5%	25%	70%
Human being	36%	13%	51%

these three means of oxygen storage in the Adélie penguin, Weddell seal, and human being.

Penguins have a very effective respiratory system, similar to that of *Ratitae*.

They can extract from each breath 50 percent oxygen, compared with 15 percent in other mammals. They have a large gas-exchange surface due to very fine blood capillaries.

Air is made of 21 percent oxygen and 79 percent nitrogen. Nitrogen is not involved in tissue respiration, but it is nonetheless present in the blood.

As penguins dive, their bodies are subjected to increased pressure, and consequently the amount of gas dissolved in the tissues rises within the same given volume. Within a 33-foot (10-m) water column, the body is subjected to pressure twice as high as on the surface.

As they return to the surface, the diminishing pressure allows the nitrogen dissolved during the dive to decompress. If they climb too quickly, nitrogen bubbles occur, leading to decompression sickness, which can result in tissue damage.

Penguins must gauge the exchange between the air sacs and the blood in order to make use of oxygen, while limiting the increase in the partial pressure of nitrogen. Most dives are short (less than 2 minutes) and shallow (less than 230 feet, or 70 m). The exchange between the lungs and the blood during the breathing process occurs at a pressure equivalent to a 225-foot (68-m) water column, in other words, at a hydrostatic pressure equivalent to 7.8 ATM.

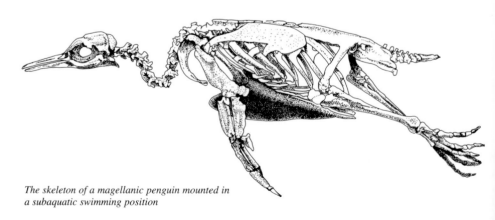

The skeleton of a magellanic penguin mounted in a subaquatic swimming position

Adélie penguins are rarely subjected to nitrogen-saturation problems. The absence of air in the bones and cranial sinuses, essential for flight, results in flattened bones with no hollow spaces, thereby reducing the amount of nitrogen stored in the body.

Penguins have a higher breathing capacity than other birds and larger gas-exchange surfaces, which enable them to quickly eliminate excess nitrogen and store oxygen when they return to the surface.

During forced submersions, Adélie penguins show an intense bradycardia (slowing of the heart rate) from 210 to 50 beats per minute in the first seconds of submersion, followed by a tachycardia (relatively rapid heart action) during decompression.

Bradycardia redistributes blood flow to essential tissues (brain, spinal cord) and restricts flow to nonessential tissues (viscera). Thus, the penguin conserves its precious combustible, not knowing how long it will be underwater.

Studies of emperor penguins during voluntary dives show no change in heart rate. The amount of oxygen needed for diving is calculated from the bird's basal metabolism and the stress generated by underwater activity (speed, heat loss). The ratio of stored oxygen to oxygen required gives us an estimated aerobic dive limit (ADL). However, there can be a disparity between the estimated ADL and the observed duration of a dive, as in the case of a free-diving emperor that remained underwater for 18 minutes, far exceeding its estimated ADL of 4.5 minutes. This same disparity occurs in Weddell seals.

Studies show that when *Phocidae* (the family of seals) exceed their aerobic dive limit, they must rely on anaerobic metabolism, which leads to a buildup of lactic acid. Lactic acid is a waste generated by the breakdown of glucose without oxygen. It is metabolized during recovery periods on the surface. The longer the dive, the longer the recovery period.

Leptonychotes weddelli need 60 minutes to metabolize lactic acid buildup after a 45-minute dive.

Emperor penguins challenge present theories once again with recovery periods between two long dives much shorter than the time needed to eliminate the metabolite. Sea elephants also are able to do repeated long dives with short recovery periods. However, there is more fascinating research yet to be done.

Even though most penguins dive less than 333 feet (100 m) for no more than two minutes on the average, the pressure to which they are exposed and their capacity to remain underwater rank them higher as diving animals than most *Otariidae* (the family of seals with external ears). The Galápagos fur seal (*Arctocephalus galapagoensis*) weighs the same as an emperor penguin, but its average dive depth is 100 feet (30 m) and average dive duration is no more than 7.7 minutes.

Thermoregulation

Penguins live in two thermally different environments: air and water. They had to adapt physiologically and behaviorally in order to cope with both. Adaptations vary with their location, from the Antarctica ice pack to the equator.

Penguins are homeothermic animals. They must maintain a body temperature between 95° and 105.8° F (35° and 41° C) to avoid irreversible damage. Thus, they have developed an elaborate means of thermoregulation that enables them to withstand thermic constraints.

A range of ambient temperatures, or a thermoneutral range, can be established for penguins at rest. Their metabolic rate remains stable within this range. Windchill is an important factor for polar species.

Physiological Adaptations

Penguins avoid heat loss by insulating themselves from outside temperatures, first, by means of a dense plumage. The feathers overlap partially, like tiles, increasing waterproofing qualities. This waterproofing is further increased by the secretion of oil from the large uropygeal gland at the base of the tail. Penguins spend a lot of time preening. They use their bill and feet to adjust and carefully oil each feather with the oily secretion. Downy aftershafts at the base of the feathers trap air and effectively prevent heat loss.

Penguins also insulate themselves by means of a thick layer of blubber with poor heat-conduction qualities. They can immerse themselves like thermos bottles in icy waters and endure polar temperatures. The efficiency of this feather-air-fat insulation decreases as the water pressure increases. The air escapes and the penguin must remain very active in order to maintain its body temperature.

In addition to this protective envelope, penguins possess a very elaborate circulatory system that regulates with great precision the irrigation of their extremities and body surface. The proximity of their arteries and veins prevents heat loss in the extremities through a heat transfer from warm, outflowing arterial blood to cold, inflowing venous blood. This countercurrent heat exchange helps to maintain the extremities at a minimal temperature and raises the temperature of the blood returning to the heart so that it is never cold. In the water, the flippers and feet are at ambient temperature or slighly higher. On land, this physiological adaptation enables emperors to tolerate air temperatures as low as 14° F (-10° C) with 10.8 mile-per-hour (18 km/h) winds without showing an increase in metabolism or a change in behavior.

The countercurrent heat exchange in penguins occasionally exposed to higher temperatures is bypassed through a large vein. The blood flow to the flippers is increased through vasodilation, and they are able to release a greater amount of heat.

The surface of the flippers in relation to the size of the penguin is directly related to the average temperatures in the species' distribution range.

Penguins release heat through other parts of the body. The *Spheniscus* species, from Peru, South Africa, and the Galápagos Islands, have highly vascuralized bare patches around the eyes and bill that allow them to dissipate excess heat. The *Eudyptes* species also have pink patches, except for *E. pachyrhynchus*, but not as pronounced. At high temperatures, the bare skin swells from the blood rushing in. In intense heat, blood vessels in the blubber swell and feathers are fluffed up to increase heat loss by convection.

Every year, new feathers grow beneath the shafts of the old ones and gradually push them out. This prevents gaps from occurring in the plumage. Year-old feathers fall as soon as the new ones are long enough to provide enough insulation.

At sea as on land, penguins rely on shivering thermogenesis to maintain body temperature. The increased metabolism burns up stored fat.

When temperatures are very low, inhaling frigid air could potentially chill the animal. However, incoming air is warmed by the blood that flows through the mucous membrane lining the nasal passages, and warm outgoing air releases heat before being exhaled. The cooling of this moist air condenses most of the vapor, thus decreasing chances of dehydration.

When temperatures are high, penguins also cool off by opening their bill wide and panting. According to the studies of Chappell and Souza on Adélie penguins, the number of inhalations per minute increases as ambient temperature rises: 8.4 inhalations per minute at 4° F (-20° C) versus 54.1 at 86 °F (30° C).

Behavioral Adaptations

When temperatures become unbearable, the penguin increases metabolic heat production through shivering thermogenesis or adapts its behavior and seeks shelter from the elements.

Emperor penguins, which are often exposed to temperatures less than their lower critical temperature of 14° F (-10° C), were forced to develop a most unusual social behavior in order to maintain a constant metabolic rate. Unlike other species that are territorial by nature, emperors huddle together on their breeding sites to form what appears to be a giant turtle. This living huddle is virtually blizzard-proof.

The group begins to form with two penguins standing side by side and a third one facing them with its head between their shoulders. Once the base of the huddle is formed, others graft themselves onto the formation. This living mass moves as a whole: the center penguins are pushed out to the periphery, while those on the periphery move toward the middle. Everyone gets a chance to warm up in the center. These huddles can comprise 200 to 300 birds when not incubating, and between 5,000 and 6,000 during incubation.

Penguins develop a huddling behavior as chicks in their crèches. Species in warm climates nest in rock crevices and under vegetation to protect their chicks from the heat of the sun. In New Zealand, fiordland penguins seek humidity under bushes. Little penguins avoid the heat of the day by waiting until night to come ashore. Other species, such as king and magellanic penguins, cool off in streams, torrents, puddles, and ponds, seeming to enjoy a nice freshwater bath.

Locomotion

Penguins are amphibious birds that feed only at sea. Their morphology has adapted perfectly to the marine environment, making them effective at locating and catching prey. However, they breed on land, and certain species (emperors and Adélies) travel great distances to and from their rookeries. Penguins are so well adapted to the sea that they consume one-third less energy traveling underwater than on land.

A fiordland penguin returning to its nest under dense tropical foliage, South Island, New Zealand

Locomotion on Land

Penguins move on land by walking, tobogganing, and jumping. Their waddling gait has been imitated and exagerated countless times, but it never ceases to amuse people of all ages. Penguins have short legs set far back on the body. This is why they look like they are about to topple over when they walk (particularly the gentoo). They walk with flat feet like plantigrade animals, such as bears and badgers.

With such a morphology, they can only trudge along, step by step. The tracks of the gentoo show clearly how the body rotates: the tail, acting as a stylet, traces a perfect sine curve in the sand framed by two parallel lines. But such a waddling gait is energetically expensive.

Emperor penguins travel several hundred miles every year. When they return to the breeding site in the fall at an average speed of 0.9 miles per hour (1.5 km/h) across some 60 miles (100 km) of pack ice, they weigh more than 88 pounds (40 kg). Their waddle is very pronounced because of their increased weight. Four months later, they return to sea to feed. They leave their chicks once their weight drops to 50.5 pounds (23 kg). This is an optimal weight that enables them to conserve enough fat to last them until they return but also to save energy to compensate for each lost pound.

When traveling a long distance, emperors take turns walking and tobogganing. Most penguins travel both ways but for different reasons. Lying down on their belly, they push with their flippers and feet, one foot after the other (see the illustration of a magellanic's tracks, right).

Adélies, living in snowy and icy regions, toboggan depending on the slope and snow resistance. By sliding on powdery snow, they avoid sinking in, conserve energy, and move faster. However, their plumage, crucial to good underwater propulsion, gets damaged in the process. Although they conserve energy traveling on land, they do spend extra time and use up additional calories preening.

Some penguins, such as magellanic and little penguins, toboggan just to escape, and only if the sandy or gravelly substratum is smooth enough. They move faster than a human walking and are able to slide over obstacles, like tussock grass (see appendix) and small crevices.

Rockhoppers, as their name indicates, bounce with their feet together. Living on rocky shores and cliffs, they sometimes hop up steps as high as they are. Their powerful feet and sharp claws help them cling onto the rocks. Macaronis also hop but not as often or as nimbly.

Locomotion at Sea

The penguins' morphology is of greatest value at sea. Built like torpedoes and covered in overlapping feathers as fine as scales, penguins fly underwater. Their slightly positive buoyancy enables them to float effortlessly, yet they can dive just as easily. Millions of years of evolution have equipped them with two efficient flippers that they use to propel them-

Tracks of a magellanic penguin as it toboggans, using its feet and flippers to propel itself

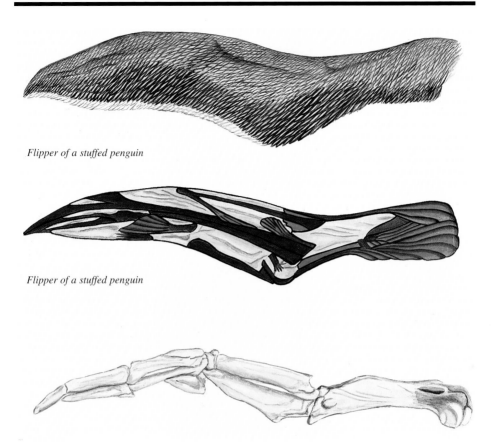

Flipper of a stuffed penguin

Flipper of a stuffed penguin

Bone structure

selves. Their adaptation to the marine environment has converged with that of seals and sea turtles.

Penguins are astoundingly agile underwater. Their flexible body enables them to change directions at vertiginous speeds. They use their bill, feet, and tail to negotiate hairpin turns as quickly or quicker than most fish they are pursuing. Their stiff flippers beat only up and down, activated by powerful dorsal muscles. Foraging occurs in three phases: diving, feeding, and returning to the surface. Penguins dive quickly at a 45° angle to increase their foraging range. Depending on their diet, they either feed gluttonously by snatching up prey left and right, or pursue isolated animals one at a time.

Foraging sites are not always located near the shore. Adults often must travel vast distances to feed their chicks. During these long hauls, they alternate among shallow dives (common among the *Spheniscus* species), surface swimming, and porpoising (leaping in and out of the water like porpoises).

Underwater swimming is the fastest and most common way of traveling. Emperors travel at an average speed of 4.3 miles per hour (7.2 km/h) but can move as fast as 10.8 miles per hour (18 km/h). Underwater swimming is also the most energy-efficient method, unless there are turbulences; then porpoising becomes the most effective means of travel.

All penguins porpoise when traveling a long distance (except for the *Spheniscus*

25

species). This enables them to keep a laminar flow along their plumage and therefore move more efficiently. They leap in and out of the water, forming a sine wave on both sides of the surface.

But even this most efficient method of propulsion and near-perfect hydrodynamics doesn't explain how penguins can swim so fast.

Surface swimming, with most of the body submerged and the tail and head out of the water, is not energy-efficient nor used for long-distance travel. Penguins don't paddle with their feet the way ducks do, but with their flippers. Their average surface-swimming speed is only 0.9 miles per hour (1.5 km/h).

A magellanic penguin crawling onto the sandy beach, Falkland Islands

Magellanics swimming with ease over the waves of the South Atlantic

Adélie penguins porpoising to their foraging grounds in the waters off the Antarctic Peninsula

27

SPECIES

Genus *Aptenodytes*

This genus used to comprise *Spheniscus, Pygoscelis,* and *Eudyptula* penguin species. *Aptenodytes* is a Greek word meaning "wingless diver."

The first engravings of the king penguin date back to 1775, after Cook's voyage, but it wasn't until Scott's first expedition (1903–1905) that an emperor breeding site was discovered.

The two species that now belong to the *Aptenodytes* genus—emperor and king—are the most familiar to the general public. Their waddling gait delights people of all ages. Their black-and-white frock coats and orange head patches have been drawn repeatedly by children around the world.

They have been described so often in popular works and children's books that some may think they are the only penguin species, and that the emperor penguin—ice emperor—is *the* penguin.

In fact, emperors and kings are far from being the standard penguin model, if there is any such thing. They are the tallest and heaviest of all. They don't build nests but rather incubate their single egg on their feet inside an abdominal fold.

Gregarious by nature, they gather by the thousands in rookeries, where their loud trumpeting is heard.

Their morphology is similar, but their habitats and breeding cycles are different. King penguins are scattered across subantarctic regions, whereas emperors live on the icy coasts of Antarctica.

Their breeding biology is different from other penguins because of their size and the short austral summer that doesn't always allow them to breed successfully.

A sample of the immense king penguin colony on Crozet Island

KING PENGUIN

Aptenodytes patagonica
Aptenodytes patagonicus
(Miller, 1778)

French: Manchot royal
German: Königspinguin
Spanish: Pinguin real, pingüino rey
Norwegian: Kongepingvin
Flemish: Koningspinguïn

Description. *Adults:* The king penguin has a rounded body with characteristic black-and-white markings enhanced by orange auricular patches.

A narrow black border separates the white underparts from the blue-gray back. The head and chin are black with a bright-orange, comma-shaped ear patch that thins out on the throat. The gradual shades of orange of the throat contrast with the pure-white breast.

The bright-pink patch on the mandible is larger than that on the emperor. The underside of the flippers is white with a black tip. The feet are black.

The king penguin is smaller than the emperor, and its orange ear patch is much brighter.

Immatures: The immature has not developed all of its colors. The auricular patches are lemon yellow, and the chest is pure white. The pink mandibular patches are not as bright and visible. Its colors develop fully at the end of the second year.

Chicks: The chick develops an immature plumage right before leaving the colony. It spends the winter clothed in thick, chocolate-brown down that it grows after leaving its parent's abdominal fold.

The chick is naked when it hatches. Soon after, a layer of down forms on its black skin, protecting it against the cold.

Length/Weight: Adults measure between 34 and 38 inches (85 and 95 cm). Males are generally taller than females. The weight of breeding adults varies from colony to colony. In the Crozet Islands males weigh about 28.1 pounds (12.8 kg) and females 25.3 pounds (11.5 kg), whereas in South Georgia they weigh respectively 35.2 pounds (16 kg) and 31 pounds (14.1 kg). Adults may weigh nearly 44 pounds (20 kg) before molting.

Breeding. The king penguin's breeding cycle is unlike any other penguin's. It breeds twice every three years. Each cycle lasts 14 to 16 months, and consists of:
two to three weeks, foraging after breeding
two to three weeks, molting on land
two to three weeks, foraging to build up reserves
two to three weeks, courting
eight weeks, incubating
40 to 59 weeks, rearing chicks

King penguins lay their egg anytime between November and March, depending on the colony.

The breeding cycle of the king penguin can be summarized as follows: The chick hatched from an egg laid in November 1992 fledges in December 1993. The parents can breed again in February 1994, and the new chick will fledge in February 1995. By the time they molt, it is too late for the next brood to produce a new fledgling, so the parents will have to wait until November 1995 for the next viable cycle.

Rookeries are located on barren ground in shallow valleys, moraines, beaches, or open areas leveled by humans. In the Crozet Islands, where the penguins' rookery had been disturbed by road construction, a piece of land was leveled to provide them with a favorable breeding site. In the Falklands, penguins cohabitate with sheep on pastureland. King penguins often live near colonies of gentoo penguins (*Pygoscelis papua*). It is not unusual to find vagrant kings living amid the gentoos.

As soon as breeding adults arrive at the rookery, they try to attract a mate by opening their flippers wide and trumpeting with their bill pointed upward. This resounding call becomes louder with each pulsation. Once a penguin of the opposite gender answers, they pair off. Facing each other, they synchronize their calls; then they do a little two-step, waddling one behind the other. After engaging in mutual display, they mate.

A king sleeping with its egg incubating under its abdominal fold

The king penguin, like the emperor, doesn't build a nest. The single egg is balanced on the adult's feet and incubated in an abdominal fold. King penguins are territorial, but only within pecking distance of the incubating parent, generally 2.6 to 3.3 feet (0.8 to 1 m).

The female lays a whitish egg that weighs a little more than 10.5 ounces (300 g). A few hours later, she passes it to her mate, although the egg sometimes breaks during the delicate transfer. The male incubates the egg for 19 days on the average. Then the parents take turns every two to three weeks for 52 to 57 days until the egg hatches.

Chick-Rearing. The chick stays in the parents' abdominal fold for the first week. Parents take turns brooding their young, as they did the egg. Now and then, the chick sticks its little head out to swallow the regurgitated food that its parents bring. The chick spends the next week in its parents' protective care, although it is already covered with its first layer of brown down.

Chicks leave their parents and gather in crèches when they are two weeks old. They are fed frequently and gain weight rapidly. When the parent returns from the sea, it lets out a unique call, and the chick answers with sharp trills that only its parents can recognize.

But these days of plenty don't last. The parents visit less frequently as the days go by. Left to their own fate, the little balls of chocolate-brown down huddle together in their crèches to protect themselves against the subantarctic winter and predators. Snowstorms and violent winds spare only the strongest, who were well fed during the first weeks. Only about 50 percent survive.

The parents return to feed their chicks only three or four times during the five winter months. Unlike emperors, king adults don't huddle during blizzards. Each parent spends several days in the crèche before heading out to sea for several weeks.

In October, when the weather is milder, they return frequently and regularly to prepare their offspring to fledge. During this period, the chick's weight increases rapidly.

Chicks are fed every four to six days. Sheathbills (*Chionis alba*) try to steal the hard-earned regurgitated food that the parents bring. It takes adults about eight days to reach foraging grounds, feed, and return to the colony.

When the chicks are 43 to 60 weeks old (depending on the colony), they shed their furry down and put on a coat resembling that of the adults.

King penguins copulating, Falkland Islands

A sheathbill stealing food out of a king chick's bill, Crozet Island

An unexpected sight: king penguins and sheep cohabiting at Volunteer Beach in the Falkland Islands

Soon they fledge, and will return only three years later to breed. Their second-year molt rarely occurs on their breeding ground.

Foraging. For a long time, researchers thought that king penguins ate only cephalopods, but studies conducted in different sites show that the species' diet varies with the season and the location.

In the Crozet Islands, the summer diet consists of fish (*Electrona carlsberghi, Krefftichthys anderssoni*) and cephalopods (*Kondakovia longimana*) and the winter diet mostly of cephalopods (48.4 percent of the food intake).

In South Georgia, cephalopods (*Psychroteutis glacialis, Martiala hyaddesi*)

comprise 90 percent of the breeding-season diet, supplemented with fish, such as *Notothenia rossi*.

Diet

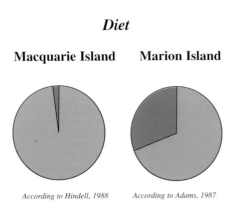

According to Hindell, 1988   According to Adams, 1987

The type of cephalopods and fish found around the Crozet Islands is also found in the waters surrounding Macquarie Island, and in similar ratios. However, *E. carlsberghi* is present mostly in winter.

On Marion Island, during the feeding season, such fish as *E. carlesberghi* and *K. anderssoni* comprise 68.7 percent of the diet, supplemented with 31.3 percent cephalopods, such as *Moroteuthis* and *K. longimana*. In winter, as in the Crozet Islands, fish species dwindle and cephalopods predominate the diet.

The size of the prey varies between 0.8 to 7.2 inches (20 to 180 mm).

Feeding habits also vary with the prey. King penguins of South Georgia chase isolated squid, whereas those of the Crozet Islands attack small fish shoals.

Chick-feeding adults stay within 180 miles (300 km) of the colony, and travel back and forth at about 5.25 miles per hour (8.7 km/h). They forage at different depths, depending on the prey and the site: 330 to 990 feet (100 to 300 m) around the Crozet Islands, and about 165 feet (50 m) in South Georgia with a maximum recorded depth of 825 feet (250 m). They dive 100 to 150 times a day for six to seven minutes each time.

Survival. Eggs, though well protected, are vulnerable to disturbances, such as a wave flooding the beach or a helicopter flying over. The breeding process can be ruined if the king penguin drops its precious load in a panic. This type of accident can seriously impact the size of the colony.

Chicks, particularly the sickly and undernourished, are under constant attack during the winter months by giant petrels (*Macronectes sp.*) or skuas (*Catharacta sp.*).

Adults, on the other hand, are most vulnerable at sea. Killer whales (*Orcinus orca*) sometimes come to snatch them in the *Laminaria* (the family of dark-spored seaweed) growing along the shore. Occasionally sea leopards (*Hydrurga leptonyx*) skin the penguins with their sharp teeth and leave their hide floating on the surface of the water, turned inside out like a sock, with the head and flippers still attached. Austral sea lions (*Otaria byronia*) attack penguins in the same way, but on the shoreline between the waves and the sand.

Distribution. The northern limit of the king penguin's breeding range is around 45° south latitude, and the southern limit is the Antarctic Convergence (although it may reach farther south in certain areas). Colonies are distributed on islands in the South Atlantic Ocean and Indian Ocean, between 46° and 55° south latitude. Stragglers have been spotted south of Australia, in Tasmania, New Zealand, and South Africa. Some have even been found breeding in South America.

The Volunteer Beach colony (East Falkland) returned recently to its breeding sites and is starting to migrate to new sites, such as Sea Lion Island (see "The Exploitation of Penguins").

Population. The breeding population comprises nearly 1,200,000 pairs. The largest colonies are on the French, subantarctic Crozet and Kerguelen Islands, followed by those of Prince Edward and Macquarie Islands. There are 188,000 king penguin pairs in South Georgia. The king population is growing throughout its range, especially in areas ravaged by hunters during the 18th and 19th centuries.

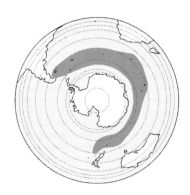

EMPEROR PENGUIN

Aptenodytes forsteri
(Gray, 1844)

French: Manchot empereur
German: Kaiserspinguin
Spanish: Pingüino emperador
Norwegian: Keiserpingvin
Flemish: Keizerspinguïn

Description. *Adults:* The top of the emperor penguin's head and chin are black. The back is a bluish gray-black, and the underparts and underside of the flippers are pure white. A narrow black border runs from the neck along the leading edge of the flippers. Beautiful yellow patches on each side of the neck fading to pale yellow on the upper breast adorn their formal plumage. The top of the bill is black with a pink-orange band on the mandibles. The feet are black.

Immatures: Immatures have a gray-blue back and head. The chin is white, unlike adults'. They have not yet developed the yellow auricular patches. The bill is black and white.

Chicks: Chicks are glabrous (hairless) when they hatch. Their skin is gray. A few weeks later, they are covered in ash-gray down. A black band runs from the back of the head to the bill, resembling a cap. This black marking grows until it covers the entire back at fledging. The rest of the head is white, with black around the eyes.

Length/Weight: Emperors are the largest of all penguins. Adults measure between 44 and 52 inches (110 and 130 cm).

Their weight varies with the gender and the season. Early in the breeding season, before a four-month fast, males weigh an average of 83.6 pounds (38 kg); 120 days later, their weight drops to 50.6 pounds (23 kg). Females fast for 45 days; their weight drops 22 percent from 63.8 pounds (29 kg) to 50.6 pounds (23 kg).

Breeding. Around March through April, the first breeders, which are at least three years old, return to their breeding site after a long trudge over the ice pack.

The ideal site is an ice pack tucked away in a bay between islands and shielded from violent winds by icebergs, rocks, or ice cliffs. However, one emperor colony breeds on dry land in a cirque formed by Taylor Glacier (Kemp Land).

Compelled by the same breeding instinct, adults trudge across the ice in a long procession and gather by the millions far from the edges of the ice pack at the beginning of the austral winter. They take turns walking and tobogganing, moving at an average speed of 0.9 miles per hour (1.5 km/h). Emperors are not territorial and don't build nests.

Male and female emperors engage in a series of vocalizations and mutual displays quite different from other penguins'. They let out a sequence of "ah-ah-ah-ah..." with their head bowed down. This call is preceded by an unusual behavior, in which they spread their flippers and rub their bill on the underside of the flippers. Penguins take turns engaging in this display so that their calls don't overlap. If one starts a fraction of a second after a neighbor standing within a 23-foot (7-m) radius, it stops and starts again after that one is done.

When a female arrives at the breeding

site, she chooses a male by standing in front of him and inviting him to join her in a series of synchronized calls. Then they start waddling along in rhythm, the male behind the female. Before copulation, they face each other and bow several times. After these preliminary displays, which can take quite long, the male stands behind the female and rubs his bill on her shoulder to get her to lie down.

These displays and calls allow emperors to memorize the vocal characteristics of their mate. It will enable them to recognize each other when they return to the colony after foraging. Emperors have no geographic landmarks or physical attributes to help them recognize their mate, and rely on calls for individual recognition.

Emperor penguins are not aggressive like other species. An emperor may peck or slap another bird only if it approaches it within neck's reach while it is brooding. Occasionally, a nonbreeder tries to steal the egg or chick as it is being passed from one parent to the other. Even if it succeeds, it soon abandons the egg, which is lost forever.

In May, the female lays a single egg that weighs an average of 15.4 ounces (440 g). She has just fasted for 40 days, spent a lot of energy producing her only egg, and must return to the sea to forage. She transfers the egg to the male by laying it on the ice, and then the male skillfully rolls it onto his feet with his bill. After that, he covers it in a fold of abdominal skin and incubates it for 62 to 65 days.

Incubation takes place during the Antarctic winter. The male is exposed to the worst weather conditions: winds up to 108 miles per hour (180 km/h) and temperatures as low as -79.6° F (-62° C). Adults gather in huddles to survive the most violent storms.

Chick-Rearing. The male is the first one to feed the chick with a milky substance rich in lipid and protein, which he secretes after a 110-day fast. After returning to the colony, the female

Emperors gathered in huddles under harsh weather conditions, Adélie Land

guards the chick for 24 days, and the male returns to the sea to feed.

When he comes back, they call out as they did while courting, only this time, to recognize each other. Then the female returns to sea for another week.

Thirty-five to 40 days after hatching, chicks are able to regulate their body temperature and leave the incubating fold. They are fed by both parents, which can now go foraging together. As summer approaches and the ice pack begins to break, the distance between the breeding site and the feeding grounds decreases.

Chicks are now fed daily or every other day, until they are ready to fledge in late November through early December, depending on the colony. They huddle like adults while their parents are away and thus are able to withstand the harsh weather conditions.

In early November, the chicks molt and put on their juvenile plumage.

In late November through early December, when they are 120 to 150 days old, they head out to sea and disperse. Unlike immatures from other species that leave their colony plump and sometimes larger than adults, emperor juveniles leave weighing only 33 pounds (15 kg) or so, half the adult weight. They are not handicapped by their lower weight, however, because the Antarctic waters in spring offer an abundant supply of fish, crustaceans, and cephalopods to help them grow. Immatures from other species fledge at the end of the summer and miss out on such favorable conditions.

This large penguin has chosen to endure the rigors of the Antarctic winter to enable its chicks to fledge at the beginning of summer.

Once the chick is raised, the adults can build up their own fat reserves. This is especially important as they are due for a second fast that will last 30 to 40 days, from November to January, while they molt.

Foraging. Emperors' feeding habits vary with the site. Studies were conducted in three sites during chick-feeding in the spring (October and November).

Diet

Weddell Sea   **Adélie Land**

According to Klages, 1989   *According to Offredo and Ridoux, 1986*

% of mass	Pointe Geologie Adélie Land	Amanda Bay McRobertson Land	Drescher Inlet Weddell Sea
Fish	95	97	38
Crustaceans	2	0.3	52
Cephalopods	3	2.7	10

The egg of Aptenodytes *is protected in an abdominal fold.*

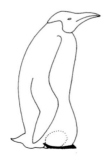

Fish, such as *Pagothenia borchgrevincki* (Adélie Land), *Pleurogramma antarcticum* (Amanda Bay), and *Notolepsis coatsi* (Drescher Inlet), dominate the diet.

In the Weddell Sea, krill (*Euphausia superba*) is the predominant crustacean. Krill measure between 1.2 and 8 inches (30 and 200 mm).

Excellent divers, emperors chase their prey at a high speed of up to 10.8 miles per hour (18 km/h). They hunt under the sea ice by alternating shallow dives with deep dives as far as 875 feet (265 m). The average duration of the dive is 2.5 to 9 minutes, with 18-minute peaks.

When they return to sea after a four-month fast (for males) or two-month fast (for females), emperors take advantage of cracks in the ice bank and seal breathing holes to fish under the sea ice.

Once they reach the edges of the ice pack, they break up into small groups and disperse within a 180-mile (300-km) perimeter (Ross Sea).

Foraging trips in Adélie Land last about three and a half days in October and only three days in November, because the penguins have better access to the open sea.

Survival. Unlike in other species, immature emperors are not attacked constantly by predatory birds, because the harshness of the austral winter keeps them away from the Antarctic continent. Only giant petrels *(Macronectes sp.)* attack chicks that wander away from their crèche. Adults and immatures are vulnerable to killer whales *(Orcinus orca)* and leopard seals *(Hydrurga leptonyx)* at the edge of the ice pack.

Eggs balanced on adults' feet can be lost when they gather in huddles during the winter. Frustrated nonbreeding penguins also can interfere with breeding when they try to snatch another penguin's egg. If the egg gets away from the brooding parent, it is hard for it to roll the egg back onto its feet, and the egg freezes quickly. Occasionally, the thief succeeds, only to soon abandon the egg or chick.

Undernourishment also accounts for many deaths among chicks. The distance between the colony and the open sea determines feeding frequency. The larger the ice pack, the longer the foraging trips. If the female does not return in time, the male is forced to leave the chick and head out to sea. September blizzards cause many such deaths, because undernourished or isolated chicks cannot survive alone in the icy Antarctic winds and freeze to death very quickly.

Distribution. Distributed in icy Antarctica, emperor colonies range from 67° to 77° south latitude. Only one colony is located near the Antarctic Peninsula, on Dion Island (67° 52' S.). Immatures also visit the eastern shores of the Falkland Islands.

Emperors have been spotted at sea near the southern tip of New Zealand, in the Kerguelen Islands, and in South Georgia.

Population. There are an estimated 195,400 emperor penguin pairs. The Ross Sea is home to more than a quarter of all breeding adults, with the largest colony of 22,137 pairs located on Coulman Island. The population is stable in spite of disturbances from nearby scientific bases. Breeders are distributed throughout 42 known colonies. The colony in Adélie Land on Pointe Geologie archipelago had more than 2,517 breeding pairs in 1986, representing less than half the pairs recorded in 1952 during the first census.

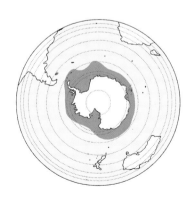

Genus *Eudyptes*

Nature once again has proven to be highly imaginative. It has crowned the austere black-and-white plumage of *Eudyptes* penguins with eccentric crests of bright-yellow feathers. Their distinctive aigrettes, short and stiff or long and undulating, are unique among penguin genera.

Eudyptes means "good diver" in Greek. This genus comprises six species, representing more than a third of all penguin species. In French, penguins in this genus are called *gorfous,* from the Scandinavian *goirfulg,* which was the name given to the great auk (*Alca impennis*) from the North Atlantic that became extinct at the beginning of the 19th century.

This prolific genus inhabits most austral islands located between 37° and 57° south latitude. New Zealand offers the most variety, with four species.

Rookeries are generally buzzing like beehives with several thousand individuals on steep, tumbling, rocky slopes.

On land, crested penguins are particularly noisy, and the raucous and shrill cries of breeding adults resound throughout the colonies. They are aggressive and feisty, and adults protect their offspring with fierceness. Crested penguins lay two eggs. Unlike with other penguin species, the first egg is smaller than the second, and is seldom incubated until hatching. Their breeding grounds offer little material for elaborate nest-building, so a pebble-filled hollow is as comfortable as it gets. Some New Zealand species build their nests under vegetation and form loose colonies in wet rain forests. After their post-breeding molt, crested penguins generally migrate.

Rockhoppers on the spurs of a crater on Saint Paul Island

FIORDLAND PENGUIN

Eudyptes pachyrhynchus
(Gray, 1845)

Also called: New Zealand crested penguin, thick-billed penguin
French: Gorfou des fjordland
German: Dickschnabelpinguin
Norwegian: Skogpingvin
Flemish: Nieuwzeelandse kuifpinguin, dikbekpinguïn
Maori: Tauake, tawaki

Description. *Adults:* The fiordland penguin has golden-yellow aigrettes sometimes punctuated by black feathers, a blue-black back, and white underparts. The adults are distinguishable from other crested penguins by their white cheek feathers and thinner bill. The underside of their flippers is lighter than that of the Snares Island penguin *(E. robustus).*

Males have a thicker bill and longer flippers and tend to be larger than females. However, their bill is not as heavy as the Snares Island penguins'.

Immatures: Immatures resemble those of neighboring species, such as *E. robustus* and *E. sclateri* (erect-crested penguin), with a blue-black back, gray chin, black head with yellow eyebrows, and brownish bill. However, fiordland immatures have no bare skin at the corner of the bill, as do Snares Island and erect-crested penguins.

Chicks: Chicks have a dark-brown back and creamy-white underparts.

Length/Weight: The average length of a fiordland is 22 inches (55 cm).

Before molting, male adults weigh an average of 10.75 pounds (4.9 kg); females, 10.55 pounds (4.8 kg). After molting, they weigh respectively 6.6 and 5.5 pounds (3 and 2.5 kg).

Breeding. The breeding season starts in the first half of June, when the first mature males (at least five years old) arrive on the nesting grounds. Living in humid forests, the crested penguins build their nests in tangles of roots or under low branches to protect their chicks from the summer heat. They also colonize tumbling, rocky shores.

They begin by building a new nest or patching last year's site with leaves (especially from the *Poa foliosa),* pebbles, and branches. Ungregarious by nature, fiordland pairs build their nests at least 6.6 feet (2 m) apart.

The male advertises his newly claimed territory by a series of trumpeting calls with his bill pointed upward and head swinging from side to side. Mated pairs engage in mutual displays, leading to copulation. During the first week in August, the female lays two different-sized eggs, four days apart. As with all *Eudyptes* penguins, the second egg is larger than the first one: 4.2 ounces (120 g) versus 3.5 ounces (100 g).

Incubation begins once the second egg is laid and lasts an average of 33.5 days. Parents take turns brooding the eggs.

Chick-Rearing. The male is responsible for guarding the chicks during their first 20 days. Meanwhile, the female goes foraging daily, returning to feed her offspring. After this first stage, chicks gather in crèches and are fed by both parents. Adults often have to make their way up steep and slippery slopes and across dense forests.

The chicks fledge in late November, when they are 75 days old. Once the breeding cycle is completed, the adults abandon the site for eight to 12 weeks to go to build up their fat reserves. They return in February through March for a monthlong molt.

Foraging. The species' feeding habits vary considerably, depending on the site. The two sites studied are close to one another: the first one is located on the southwest coast of South Island, New Zealand, and the second, on the north coast of Stewart Island.

In the first site, South Island, calamari *(Nototodarus sloanii, Moroteuthopsis ingens)* and octopus *(Ocythoe tubercula-ta, Octopus maorum)* are the main prey. *Euphausiidae* crustaceans *(Nyctiphanes australis)* are the primary supplement. Fish are eaten at a larval or post-larval stage (between 1.1 and 1.4 inches long [28 and 35 mm]).

On Stewart Island, the fish are the same size, but the main catch consists of *Auchenoceros punctatus* and *Pseudophycis bachus.*

The average stomach content on Codfish Island (near Steward Island) is 5.8 ounces (166 g), and it is 12.2 ounces (348 g) in Martin Bay on South Island of New Zealand. Chick-feeding adults forage above the continental plateau, 6 to 9 miles (10 to15 km) away from the colony. They generally return in the evening, but sometimes stay at sea overnight.

Diet

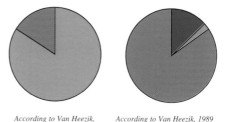

Codfish Island, NZ   Martin Bay, NZ

According to Van Heezik, 1990   According to Van Heezik, 1989

A fiordland pair sheltered in the rain forest on South Island, New Zealand

The weka, a fierce predator that attacks penguin eggs, New Zealand

Survival. An estimated 50 percent of fiordland pairs rear one chick to fledging. The species has few land predators. The only enemy is the weka *(Galliralus australis)*, which attacks eggs by sneaking through the vegetation. This *Rallidae* was introduced on Steward Island at the beginning of the century, and has played havoc ever since. Humans, always tampering with biotopes, introduced a *Mustelidae* (the family of martins, skunks, weasels, minks, and otters) that attacks eggs and chicks, and even adult penguins.

Colonies living near farms must also contend with dogs.

Distribution. The species is found in New Zealand and, as their name indicates, in the Fiordland region, from Bruce Bay to the Vert Islets on the southwest coast of South Island. They breed on Stewart, Solander, and neighboring islands. They visit the southern coasts of Australia and Tasmania regularly, when they disperse after breeding and molting.

This could actually be considered a migration. Fiordlands spend the difficult winter months at sea, leaving the rookeries deserted.

Population. There are an estimated 10,000 to 20,000 fiordland breeders. The population seems to be relatively stable and is not subjected to much human interference.

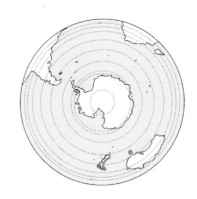

ERECT-CRESTED PENGUIN

Eudyptes sclateri
(Buller, 1888)

Also called: Sclater's penguin
French: Gorfou de Sclater
German: Kronenpinguin, Sclaterpinguin
Norwegian: Hornpingvin
Flemish: Grote kuifpinguin

Description. *Adults:* The erect-crested penguin is recognizable by its beautiful, brushlike crest that earned it its name.

The crest, or aigrette, is made of golden-yellow feathers 2.4 inches (6 cm) long. The bill is reddish brown with a conspicuous white band along the base of the mandible. The head, chin, and back are blue-black. The feet are pink.

Immatures: Immatures have a yellow eyebrow, where their erect crest will grow later. Their chin is white with gray spots. Their bill is more slender than adults' and is orange-brown. They develop an adult plumage around January through February before they fledge.

Chicks: Chicks have a dark-brown back and white underparts.

They are bulkier than their cousins. Their head is flattened vertically. This feature is accentuated by the erectness of their crest. They have the same plumage as immature Snares (*E. robustus)* and fiordland *(E. pachyrhynchus)* penguins.

Length/Weight: Erect-crested penguins measure 26.8 inches (67 cm) on the average. Their weight varies with their age and gender and the season. The average weight of a male is 10.8 pounds (4.9 kg), and can be as high as 15.4 pounds (7 kg) before molting and as low as 7.9 pounds (3.6 kg) after. The average weight of a female is 9 pounds (4.1 kg), with a high of 12.75 pounds (5.8 kg) and a low of 6.4 pounds (2.9 kg), before and after molting.

Breeding. Bounty and Antipodes Islands have rocky shores with promontories that often form little grottos. Erect-crested penguins nest in rock cavities sheltered from the intense sunlight.

The first breeders arrive on the site in early September. The male attracts a prospective mate to his nest site by vocalizing accompanied by a vertical head-swinging motion. He gathers pebbles, plants, and other debris to build the nest. He generally builds the nest himself by arranging the materials with his bill and flippers.

The male will do whatever is necessary to defend his territory, from displaying threats with his bill agape and neck outstretched while growling lightly to outright fights with pecks and flailing flippers.

Copulation occurs after a series of mutual displays and resounding vocalizations. The calls of erect-crested penguins are lower-pitched and louder than those of their cousins from New Zealand. Mutual preening of the head and neck is also common between mates, as well as between parents and chicks.

Most eggs are laid around October 12 on Antipodes Island and three weeks later on Bounty Island.

Erect-crested penguins are a gregarious species. There are 0.8 nests in every square meter on rocky ledges, where penguins can gather in greatest numbers. They sometimes share breeding grounds with rockhopper penguins *(E. chryso-come filholi)* and shy albatrosses *(Diomedea cauta).*

The two eggs vary in size like those of other crested-penguin species, with an average of 3.4 ounces (98 g) for the first egg and 5.2 ounces (149 g) for the second. Parents take turns incubating for a total of 35 days.

Chick-Rearing. The female seems more willing to feed the chicks during the first weeks of the guard stage. Chicks gather in crèches as soon as they are too big to fit between the adults' feet.

The young ones gather in the middle of the colony in a quarrelsome crèche, where they peck at each other often.

They fledge in mid-January.

The adults leave shortly after the fledglings. They stay at sea for a month to rebuild their reserves, and begin to molt when they are at their heaviest. Most of them return to the breeding site in late February through early March. It takes about 30 days to renew their plumage. Come late April, the colony will be deserted once again.

Foraging. Dietary evidence suggests that erect-crested penguins eat only cephalopods and crustaceans.

Survival. Rats, brought by boat to most islands around the world, eat the eggs of erect-crested penguins.

On Antipodes, skuas snatch eggs and chicks.

The fur seal *(Arctocephalus forsteri)* is the only pinniped that has been observed attacking this species.

Distribution. Erect-crested penguins breed regularly on Antipodes and Bounty Islands, and in small numbers on Auckland and Campbell Islands.

During the winter, the colonies are deserted, when the erect-crested penguin population disperses at sea.

Erect-crested penguins have been spotted regularly on Snares and Campbell Islands, in the southern part of Australia, and on all New Zealand shores. They occasionally visit Chatham and Macquarie Islands, and were once seen on West Point Island in the Falkland archipelago. An immature was spotted one time in the Kerguelen Islands.

Population. There are about 115,000 breeding pairs on Bounty Island and the same number on Antipodes. The population appears to be stable due to the lack of human interference.

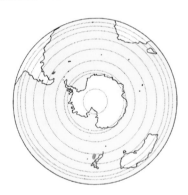

An erect-crested penguin on Antipodes Island

ROCKHOPPER PENGUIN

Eudyptes chrysocome
Aptenodytes chrysocome
(Forster, 1781)

E. c. chrysocome (Falkland and Cape
Horn Islands)
E. c. filholi (Hutton, 1879) (Marion,
Crozet, Kerguelen, Heard, Macquarie,
Campbell, Auckland, and Antipodes
Islands)
E. c. moseleyi (Matthews and Iredale,
1921) (Tristan da Cunha, Gough,
Amsterdam, and St. Paul Islands)

Also called: Crested penguin,
jumping-jack
French: Gorfou sauteur
German: Felsenpinguin
Spanish: Pingüino de penacho amarillo,
pingüino real
Norwegian: Klippehopperpingvin
Flemish: Rotspinguïn, rotsspringer
Fuegian (Yaghan): Kalanina

Description. *Adults:* The rockhopper is
the smallest crested penguin but also one
of the most robust.

The head is black; the back is blue-
black.

Yellow eyebrows fan out into a spiked
crest on each side of the head. The top of
the head is adorned with a black "crew
cut" that grows shorter toward the bill.

The yellow crest plumes of the subspecies *E. c. moseleyi* are longer and more
untidy than those of the other subspecies.
This subspecies is the largest of all three.

The subspecies *E. c. filholi* is distin-
guished by a pink, fleshy patch at the
base of the bill that sometimes reaches
under the mandible. The yellow eyebrows are larger in this subspecies. The
markings under the flippers provide
another means of identification.

The rockhopper's bill is reddish brown.
The iris is red. The feet are pink.

Immatures: Immatures molt and put on
a nearly adult plumage before fledging.
The only differences are that their chin is
gray, their bill is blue-gray, and they have
no occipital crest.

Chicks: Chicks are blue-gray (head,
back, flippers) with white underparts.

Length/Weight: Rockhoppers measure
between 18 and 23.2 inches (45 and 58
cm).

According to weights taken in the
Falklands, males can weigh as much as
9.45 pounds (4.3 kg) before molting and
as little as 5 pounds (2.3 kg) after.
Females weigh less, with a high of 8
pounds (3.65 kg) before molting and a
low of 4.85 pounds (2.2 kg) after.

The rockhopper penguin is smaller than
the macaroni penguin *(E. chrysolophus)*,
and its bill is not as strong.

Breeding. The breeding season varies
with the colony and the yearly weather
variations.

It is generally delayed 10 days for each
degree variation in sea temperature, so
the southernmost populations breed later.

In the Falkland Islands, males arrive in
early October, followed by females 10
days later. The first eggs are laid in the
first week of November and hatch in
early December.

The males start building their nest with
pebbles, leaves, or twigs as soon as they
arrive on the site. Nests are sheltered
under tussock grass or in rock fissures, or
perched on rock ledges.

Rockhoppers share breeding sites with the black-browed albatross *(Diomedea melanophrys)* or different species of cormorant *(Phalacrocorax sp.)*, so they occasionally use their unoccupied nests.

Colonies are sometimes far from the sea. For centuries, these birds have followed the same trails to return to their breeding sites after foraging at sea.

Some rockhopper colonies are located at the tops of cliffs. Highly eroded by crashing waves, these cliffs have only one way up to the breeding site and one way down to the sea. Rockhoppers often have to make several attempts to get a foothold on the slippery rocks before they can hop up the slope from rock to rock, some rocks being as high as they are.

Once the male claims his territory, he announces it through a series of pulsating calls while engaged in an ecstatic display: bill pointing to the sky, head swinging frenetically from side to side (faster than any other *Eudyptes),* and flippers open wide to reveal his black-and-white markings. The female he attracts synchronizes her calls to his.

Rockhoppers are rather aggressive birds. They defend their territory against intruders and are not afraid to chase away forceful skuas. They try to dissuade encroachers with their outstretched neck and raucous cries. If this doesn't work, they strike out with their bill and flippers, generally succeeding in scaring off a pestering neighbor or a lost chick.

As soon as the female arrives, she digs a hollow in the materials brought by the male and finishes building the very plain nest.

She lays two different-sized eggs, four to five days apart. The average weight of the first egg is between 2.5 and 2.75 ounces (76 and 79 g), and that of the second is close to 3.85 ounces (110 g). Incubation starts as soon as the second egg is laid, lasting about 35 days.

The male then returns to sea after a 34-day fast. The female incubates the eggs for 12 days or so. When the male takes over, she has just completed a 40-day fast. It takes her nine days to build up reserves. She arrives back at the nest and takes over for the remaining few days of incubation.

A rockhopper guarding its chick from violent winds in the Falkland Islands

Chick-Rearing. The chick from the second egg is generally the one to survive.

The male guards his offspring during the first three weeks. In the meantime, the female makes daily foraging trips to feed the chick. Each time she returns, she identifies herself to her mate through a series of vocalizations.

Chicks gather in crèches when they are 21 days old. The female feeds the chick for the first week, while the male goes to sea to build up his reserves after this second fast.

The couple then will share the feeding responsibility, until the chick fledges at 65 to 70 days old.

When the adult returns from the sea, it calls out to the chick, sometimes perched upon a promontory. A ball of brown-and-white down comes out of the crèche and approaches its parent, identifying itself by a distinctive whistle. If another chick approaches, the adult pushes it away with its bill. On Marion Island, the time spent at sea is proportional to the chick's age, ranging from 12 to 60 hours.

After this carefree childhood, fledglings disperse near the Subtropical Convergence, where they are able to feed themselves.

Breeding adults molt for 25 to 30 days.

Foraging. The rockhopper's diet consists mainly of planktonic crustaceans, such as *Euphasia valentinei, Euphausia lucens, Themisto gaudichaudii,* and *Themisto antarctica,* in different proportions, depending on the season and the location.

Cephalopods and fish, such as *Galitheutis glacialis, Kondakovia longimana,* and *Krefftichthys anderssoni,* provide the balance of the diet. Crested penguins feed on the most abundant species available, so their diet changes throughout the year based on the predominant prey, cephalopods in larval state or *Euphausidae* crustaceans.

On Beauchêne Island (Falklands), cephalopods *(Illex argentinus, Teuthowenia sp.)* represent more than 53 percent (in mass) of the daily food intake,

supplemented by *Euphausidae.* Each prey measures between 0.4 and 2.4 inches (10 and 60 mm).

During the breeding season, parents forage within a 15- to 30-mile (25- to 50-km) radius and sometimes go as far as 180 miles (300 km). Their average speed is 4.45 miles per hour (7.4 km/h). They move in perfectly synchronized groups.

The maximum diving depth recorded is 330 feet (100 m), although most of their prey occur closer to the surface.

Diet

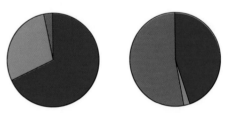

Crozet Island

According to Ridoux, personal communication

New Island

According to K. Thomson, personal communication

Macquarie Island **Beauchêne Island**

According to Hindell, 1988

According to Croxall et al., 1985

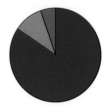

Marion Island

According to Brown and Klages, 1987

Survival. Rockhoppers are distributed over a vast territory, so predators vary with the site. On Gough Island, blue sharks *(Prionace glauca)* attack crested penguins. In the Falklands, leopard seals *(Hydrurga leptonyx)* stalk them at the base of their favorite diving rocks.

Other pinnipeds, such as fur seals *(Arctocephalus forsteri, A. australis)* and hooker sea lions *(Phocarctos hookeri),* attack adults at the edge of the water.

The striated caracara *(Phalcoboenus australis)* preys upon weak and poorly guarded chicks. If it is unable to snatch a chick, it comes back for the very same one again when it returns to the colony.

The unavoidable skua *(Catharacta sp.)* steals eggs and chicks throughout the entire colony.

Giant petrels *(Macronectes sp.)* snatch wounded and sick birds. On islands infested by rats *(Rattus norvegicus),* poorly guarded eggs are stolen quickly.

Distribution. The three rockhopper sub-species are distributed throughout three

A striated caracara having just snatched a young rockhopper from its nest

different geographical areas.

E. *chrysocome chrysocome* live in the South Atlantic, from Tierra del Fuego to Tristan da Cunha, with the largest concentration in the Falkland Islands. A few isolated birds are found on the Magellan archipelago and even on the Pacific coast.

E. *c. moseleyi* colonize Indian Ocean islands: Marion, Crozet, Kerguelen, Tristan da Cunha, and Amsterdam (which is why they are also called Amsterdam crested penguins).

The third subspecies, E. *c. filholhi,* is not as widespread. They inhabit Macquarie, Campbell, and Auckland Islands, south of New Zealand.

Population. The world population of rockhoppers is in sharp decline, so it is hard to estimate how many there are. Campbell Island offers a shocking example: the estimated number of breeders in the late 1980s was only 6 percent of the early forties population, dropping from

1,629,000 to 103,100.

The numbers are just as alarming on the Auckland Islands, where the population dropped an estimated 54 to 64 percent in less than 20 years, between 1972 and 1990.

The population estimates in the Falklands, known for their large penguin population, are just as catastrophic. In the thirties there were approximately 2.5 million pairs, and today there are only 300,000 to 400,000. And the Sea Lion

Island colony dropped from 150,000 couples in the summer of 193233 to 1,000 couples during the same season in 1991–92. Even more dramatic is the 75 percent drop in population on Beauchêne Island at the southern tip of the archipelago in just 10 years: 300,000 pairs in 1980–81 to 71,500 in 1991–92.

This decline in the rockhopper population is mainly due to famine. The lack of food may be linked to an appreciable rise in sea temperature that has led to a decrease in the krill population, the rockhoppers' predominant food source. There may be other causes, such as overfishing, more predators around like rats and cats, and illness.

It is also worth noting that in the case of Falkland penguins, egg collecting at the beginning of the century greatly impacted the size of the colonies. For example, 25,000 eggs were collected in 1915 from the 12,500 breeders on Kidney Island.

South Georgia has only 20 or so breeders.

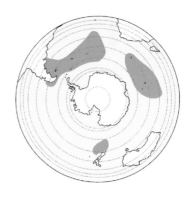

An austral sea lion chasing rockhoppers on New Island

MACARONI PENGUIN

Eudyptes chrysolophus
Catarrhactes chrysolophus
(Brandt, 1837)

French: Gorfou macaroni, gorfou doré
German: Goldschopfpinguin,
Macaronipinguin
Spanish: Pingüino macaroni, pingüino
de frente amarilla, pingüino anaranjado
Norwegian: Gulltoppingvin
Flemish: Macaronipinguïn

Description. *Adults:* More robust than
the rockhopper, the macaroni penguin is
recognizable by its golden-yellow
aigrettes and strong reddish-brown bill.
The plumes originate from a patch in the
middle of the forehead at eye level, and
they fan out into long black and yellow
feathers.

The head and throat are blue-black. The
back is bluish black. The underparts are
white, and the feet, whitish.

Some adults have a white or gray face,
which makes it hard to distinguish them
from the royal penguin *(Eudyptes
schlegeli).* Some classification experts
consider these two species one, whereas
others identify the royal as a subspecies
of the macaroni: *E. chrysolophus
schlegeli.*

Unlike the rockhopper *(E. chrysocome),*
the macaroni walks rather than hops, as
do *Pygoscelis* penguins.

Immatures: Immatures have the same
plumage as adults', except that their
throat is gray and only a few yellow eyebrow plumes are visible where the crest
will later grow. Their bill is lighter than
the adults'.

In their second year, they put on their
adult plumage but their crest is not yet as
distinct.

Chicks: The head, chin, and back are
chocolate brown. The underparts are
white, and the bill, black.

Length/Weight: Macaroni penguins

are one of the tallest *Eudyptes* species,
with an average height of 28.4 inches
(71 cm), although they can be as short as
26.4 inches and as tall as 30.4 inches.
Their weight varies considerably, depending on their annual breeding and
molting cycles.

Females are apparently heavier than
males before breeding. They expend a lot
of energy molting and lose much weight
in the process, dropping from 13.4 to 7.5
pounds (6.1 to 3.4 kg) on the average in
25 days.

Breeding. The breeding season starts in
late September in the Kerguelen Islands
and in the last week of October on Heard
Island.

First, the males arrive and immediately
set out to claim a nest site. They define
and prepare the territory for the female
by collecting pebbles, fighting off intruders, and squawking. The females arrive at
the rookery one week later. The male
tries to attract a female by engaging in an
ecstatic display. He raises his head and
points his bill skyward with his flippers
open wide, and then he lets out a raucous
and loud bray, while shaking his head
and flippers.

The pair forms and engages in mutual

preening and displays at the nest site. Facing each other, they frenetically and rhythmically shake their flippers and head, with their bill pointed upward.

Macaroni penguins gather in dense colonies. Their nests are within neck and bill reach of one another, or about 16 inches (40 cm) apart.

These megalopolis, often counting several hundred thousand birds, form on rocky slopes, rock ledges, and cliff tops.

Macaronis sometimes share breeding sites with rockhoppers. The little breeding groups from the South Shetlands join chinstrap penguin *(Pygoscelis antarctica)* colonies.

The female lays two whitish eggs: the first, a week after she arrives at the site, and the second, about four days later. The second egg weighs approximately 40 percent more than the first: about 5.4 ounces (154 g) (on Heard Island).

Incubation lasts 35 days after the second egg is laid. Both partners share duties equally. The female guards the eggs for the first 12 to 14 days, while the male goes to sea after a monthlong fast. He then returns to take the second shift for 12 to 14 days. Ninety-nine percent of the time, only one egg hatches, and both parents are present for the occasion.

Chick-Rearing. The female feeds the chick during its first 20 days. The male guards it, while the female goes out to sea daily and returns with regurgitated food.

A rockhopper defends its territory from a macaroni penguin. Notice the difference in their crests and the size of the macaroni.

The parents don't visit as frequently after the chick joins the crèche. The parents bring back more food from each foraging trip, as they travel farther out to richer feeding grounds. When they return to the colony, they call out to the chick in an ecstatic display, with their bill pointed upward and flippers open wide. The chick replies with its unique little cheep. Mutual preening often follows.

Chicks fledge when they are 60 days old. The parents also go out to sea for 11 to 14 days to build up reserves, before returning to the nesting site for a 24-day molting cycle. In South Georgia, the colony is deserted by the end of April.

Foraging. The diet consists mainly of krill (92 percent in South Georgia), supplemented by fish. Farther north, around Marion Island, the menu is more varied, with crustaceans *(Euphausia vallentinei, Themisto gaudichaudii)* as the main component, supplemented by a larger amount of fish *(Krefftichtys andersoni, Protomyctophum tenisoni)* and cephalopods *(Kondakovia longimana).* According to V. Ridoux, Crozet Island birds have the same feeding-season diet. However, the ratio of crustaceans/fish/cephalopods varies seasonally, and so does the type of prey within each family. At the beginning of the breeding season, *T. gaudichaudii* represent nearly 50 percent of the crustaceans consumed, and only 10 percent three months later.

The size of the prey ranges from 0.16 to 5.04 inches (4 to 126 mm).

The weight of their stomach content varies considerably from site to site: about 9.55 ounces (273 g) on Marion Island, 24.2 ounces (692 g) in South Georgia, and 6.7 ounces (192 g) the maximum average in January in the Crozet Islands.

Recent studies in South Georgia show that macaronis forage daily and in the daytime while they are raising their young. Their foraging trips become increasingly long as the days go by. At the end of the chick-feeding stage, the adults stay out longer to capitalize on the abundant fishing in the early nighttime hours. Dives last 1.4 to 1.7 minutes at depths of 66 to 115.5 feet (20 to 35 m), with a maximum recorded depth of 379.5 feet (115 m). Nocturnal dives last on the average 0.9 minutes and don't exceed 33 feet (10 m) in depth. There can be as many as 45 dives per hour.

Generally, macaronis travel no more than 60 miles (100 km) to reach dense schools of crustaceans and cephalopods. However, some birds will travel up to 180 miles (300 km).

Foraging trips last 12 hours or so in South Georgia, but in the Crozet Islands they can last for an average of 3.5 days. On Marion Island, birds feed for 12 hours after hatching, and for 36 to 84 hours at the end of the chick-feeding stage.

Penguins porpoise at an average speed of 4.5 miles per hour (7.5 km/h) over these long distances.

Diet

Marion Island   **South Georgia**

According to Brown and Klages, 1987

According to Croxall and Prince, 1980

The female prepares a hollow in a pile of rocks by lying on it belly-down and rotating her body with her flippers.

Survival. As in most colonies, penguin eggs are skuas', sheathbills', and Dominican gulls' favorite prey. Giant petrels attack young chicks, and leopard seals prey upon macaronis at the water's edge.

There could be several reasons for the 99 percent chance of losing the first egg, such as the male's heightened aggressiveness at the beginning of the incubation period, increased predation resulting from inattentive parents, and the parents' rejection of the first egg once the second one is laid.

Distribution. Macaroni penguins are found from the coast of Chile (Diego Ramirez Island, Black Island) to the Heard and Macdonald Islands. There are none in the South Pacific.

Some inhabit the Macquarie and Campbell Islands, south of Australia. Macaronis are the southernmost *Eudyptes* species, and they nest in small groups in the South Shetland Islands: Deception Island, Elephant Island, and Livingston. Breeding pairs and stragglers are often seen on the archipelago west of

the Antarctic Peninsula. Stragglers have been spotted now and then on the Antarctic Peninsula, and breeders on Humble Island at latitude 60° 46' S.

Population. This is the second-largest species, with a breeding population estimated at more than 9,400,000 pairs.

The largest concentrations are located in South Georgia (3 million pairs), Heard Island (1 million pairs), Macdonald Island (1 million pairs), and the Kerguelen Islands (1.8 million pairs).

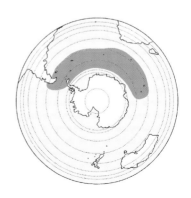

ROYAL PENGUIN

Eudyptes schlegeli
(Finsch, 1876)

French: Gorfou de schlegel, gorfou
royal
German: Haubenpinguin
Norwegian: Hvitkinnpingvin
Flemish: Macquariepinguïn, schlegel-
pinguïn

Description. *Adults:* The royal penguin
looks a great deal like its cousin, the macaroni (*Eudyptes chrysolophus*), and it is
often considered its subspecies.

Both have the same general appearance,
with a black back, white underparts, gold-
en plumes, a strong reddish-brown bill,
and a gray band separating the black-and-
white plumage. The main difference is
that the royal's face is white. However,
within the colony, there are many variations between white and black on the
face, depending on the bird's age. It is
easy to identify a royal at sea, because it
is the only white-faced penguin.

Immatures: Immatures have a grayish
face and only a few yellow plumes above
the eyes. Their bill is pinkish gray.

Chicks: Chicks have a dark-brown head
and back, and their flippers are also dark
brown. Their underparts are white.

Length/Weight: Adults measure between 26 and 30 inches (65 and 75 cm).

During chick-feeding, males weigh an
average of 9.9 pounds (4.5 kg) and
females, 8.8 pounds (4 kg). Before molting, they weigh between 11 and 13.2
pounds (5 and 6 kg).

Breeding. The colonies are encamped on
sandy or rocky beaches or on rocky slopes.

The males return to their breeding
grounds between mid-September and early
October. They gather pebbles, bones, and
all sorts of debris, and dig a little hollow in
the sand with their belly and feet.

Once they claim a new territory or
reclaim the one from the previous year,
they engage in a series of displays, with
outstretched flippers, head pointing
upward and swinging from left to right,
while braying raucously in short and long
sequences.

The same pairs often come together
from one year to the next.

Copulation begins with the male circling the female and flailing her on her
back with his flippers.

The female lays two eggs in October.
The first one weighs only 3.5 ounces
(100 g), whereas the second one weighs
up to 5.25 ounces (150 g). As soon as the
second egg is laid, the first one is pushed
out of the nest.

The female incubates the egg for the
first two weeks, and then the male takes
over for the next two. They don't hesitate
to use their bill and flippers to chase
away nosy neighbors, especially those
who had no luck in finding a mate and
are now trying to steal their egg. Both
parents are there when the chick hatches
after about 35 days of incubation.

Chick-Rearing. The female feeds the
chick during the first 20 days, while the
male guards it. She goes foraging every
day, and the chick grows rapidly.

Then it joins a crèche with chicks from
neighboring nests. The parents now are
free to go fishing together, and they
return to feed the chick every two or
three days.

When the parents return from the sea, they go back to the nest and call out to the chick, which comes out of the crèche to feed.

When chicks are five to six weeks old, they molt and start putting on their juvenile plumage. They fledge in early February. Breeding adults and immatures leave the colony shortly afterward.

Adults return to the nesting site to molt in early March, after spending five weeks out at sea building up their reserves. These reserves give the penguin the energy needed to endure the 24- to 29-day fast, during which they renew their plumage.

Come late April, they take off once again.

Foraging. Crustaceans, particularly *Euphausia valentinei,* predominate the royal's diet during the breeding season, representing 32 percent of its food intake. Another *Euphausidae, Thysanoessa gregaria,* and fish, such as *Magnesudis prionosa* and *Electronna carlesbergi,* make up the rest of the diet. Royals seldom consume cephalopods (*Moroteuthis*).

Diet

Macquarie Island

According to Hindell, 1988

Survival. The weka *(Galliralus australis),* an apterous bird, slips through the clumps of tussock grass to snatch the royals' eggs. A good walker, it travels across dunes and through tunnels formed by the dense vegetation, searching for unguarded nests. This bird was introduced on several islands, including Macquarie

Island, around 1870, and has wreaked havoc in some royal penguin colonies.

Eggs and young chicks in nests located on the periphery of the colonies cannot escape the skuas *(Catharacta lonnbergi).* Sea elephants *(Mirounga leonina)* are known to destroy eggs, chicks, and sometimes adults, as they move across nesting sites like steamrollers. New Zealand fur seals *(Arctocephalus forsteri)* also attack royals from time to time.

Distribution. Royals breed only on Macquarie Island and the surrounding islets.

Some birds have been seen on the east coast of New Zealand, in Tasmania, and in Australia on the Victoria coast. Immatures have even been spotted in Adélie Land (Antarctica).

Vagrant royals sometimes show up on Campbell and Snares Islands.

It is unclear whether the white-faced birds spotted on Crozet and Marion Islands were actually royals or macaronis *(E. chrysolophus)* with an unconventionally white face.

Population. Royals were slaughtered in great numbers during the 19th century (see "The Exploitation of Penguins") and became nearly extinct. The population on Macquarie Island was restored in 1985 to an estimated 848,700 breeding pairs.

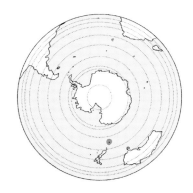

Pages 62–63: royal penguin colony at Sandy Bay on Macquarie Island

SNARES PENGUIN

Eudyptes robustus
(Oliver, 1953)

Also called: Snares crested penguin
French: Gorfou des Iles Snares
German: Snaresinselnpinguin, Snares-
Dickschnabelpinguin
Norwegian: Snarespingvin
Flemish: Grote kuifpinguïn

Description. *Adults:* The Snares penguin is similar to its neighbor, the fiordland penguin *(Eudyptes pachyrhynchus),* but stockier. It was named *Eudyptes robustus* because of the robust size of its bill. The back, head, chin, and upperside of its flippers are blue-black. It has a pinkish gape at the corner of the bill (unlike *E. pachyrhynchus).*

The yellow crest starts at the bill and forms eyebrows, before fanning out at the back of the head.

The feet are pink. The bill is reddish brown. Before molting, the plumage is brownish gray and the crest pale yellow.

Immatures: Immatures have thin, yellow eyebrows where the crest will grow later.

Their chin is gray with a white rim at the corner of the bill that is pointed slightly upward. The bill is pinkish gray. They develop their distinctive crested plumage when they are 15 months old.

Chicks: Chicks are dark brown, but their underparts and the underside of their flippers are white. At 10 days old, they put on a shorter brown down.

Length/Weight: Adults measure between 20 and 24 inches (50 and 60 cm).

The average weight of the male is 7.25 pounds (3.3 kg), whereas the female weighs 6.15 pounds (2.8 kg).

Breeding. The breeding season starts when the males arrive at the rookeries in mid-August. The females arrive a week later. On the Western Chain Islets, the cycle begins six weeks later, so the eggs are not laid until mid-November.

The males begin by claiming a nesting site, usually the same one as the previous year. They collect leaves, branches, and mud to build the nest. In barren areas, they use bones from birds. Nests are built under bushes and scrub *(Olearia lyallii* and *Brachyglottis stewartiae).*

Standing on their territory in ecstatic display, the males try to attract a female by loud calls and vertical head-swinging with flippers open wide. Bonds between males and females are maintained year after year. After a series of mutual displays with pulsating vocalizations, they copulate. Mutual preening is common, too.

The female lays two pale-blue eggs between the end of September and mid-October, four days apart. As with all *Eudyptes,* the first egg is smaller than the second, with an average weight of 3.15 ounces (90 g) versus 4.10 ounces (117 g). Incubation begins after the second egg is laid and lasts 33.4 days on the average (31 to 37 days). During the first 10 days, the parents take frequent turns incubating. After that, the female takes the first 10-day shift, and then the male takes over for the remainder of the incubation until the egg hatches. Following a five-week fast, the male returns to the sea.

Chick-Rearing. The male guards the two chicks during the first three weeks, while the female goes foraging to feed her young. Snares penguins defend their nest aggressively and try to intimidate trespassers by hissing and raising their crests. It is rare for both chicks to survive this guard stage. The survivor is usually the chick from the second egg.

It soon joins other chicks in crèches of six to 12 furry balls. Both parents are responsible for feeding the chick, but the female is the most active of the two. After a couple of days at sea, the adult returns to the colony and calls out loudly with its bill pointed skyward. The chick answers with sharp cheeps.

Around mid-January in the Snares Islands, 75-day-old immatures leave the colony, followed shortly after by the adults.

After spending two months building up their fat reserves, the adults return to the nesting site for their annual molt. It takes about a month to grow their new plumage. Then in May they all head out to sea.

Foraging. Snares penguins live mostly on crustaceans, such as *Nyctiphanes australis*. They sometimes eat cephalopods *(Nototodarus sloanii* and *Moroteuthis ingens)* and occasionally fish *(Paranotothenia magellanica).*

Snares penguins forage by day in groups of 20 along with *Procellariiformes* and *Laridae.*

Survival. Hooker's sea lions *(Phocarctos hookeri)* are Snares' main predators. They attack the penguins on the beach and skin them offshore, leaving behind their pelts, turned inside out, the way leopard seals *(Hydrurga leptonyx)* and austral sea lions *(Otaria byronia)* do.

Occasionally, leopard seals *(Hydrurga leptonyx)* and New Zealand fur seals *(Arctocephalus forsteri)* attack adults. Giant petrels *(Macronectes sp.)* take fledglings. Skuas *(Catharacta sp.)* patrol the outer edges of the colony and occasionally steal eggs.

Distribution. This species is endemic to the Snares Islands (lat. 48° S.), as its name indicates: Mainland, Broughton, and Western Chain. Snares penguins are found occasionally on the New Zealand coast, 90 miles (150 km) away, and on islands near their breeding sites.

Stragglers are sometimes found on South Island of New Zealand and on neighboring islands, such as Stewart, Chatham, Campbell, and Macquarie. On rare occasions, they have been spotted on North Island, and some even have been recorded in Australia and Tasmania. Most of these distant sightings are molting immatures.

Population. Population estimates for Snares penguins are not very accurate. Miskelly counts 33,000 breeding pairs, whereas Tennyson counts a total population of 54,000.

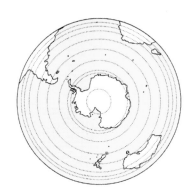

A Snares penguin couple engaged in mutual preening

Genus *Pygoscelis*

Pygoscelis is a Greek word meaning "elbow leg." The genus is composed of three species distributed south of 50° south latitude, all the way to the shores of the Antarctic continent.

They each have a distinctive marking that helps identify them. The chinstrap penguin *(P. antarctica)* has a thin black band running across its white chin. The Adélie penguin *(P. adeliae)* has standard black-and-white plumage with a white ring around the eyes. The gentoo penguin *(P. papua)* is even easier to recognize because of its orange bill and white headband and the white speckles across the top of its head.

The Adélie is the only species to breed on the Antarctic continent, but all three species are found on the islands off the Antarctic Peninsula.

These three species are poor architects: their nests are mere shallow depressions in the ground lined with pebbles.

Agonistic behavior varies with the species: gentoos react shyly when an intruder approaches their nest, chinstraps are rather fierce, and Adélies defend their territory with moderate aggressiveness.

Chinstrap penguin colony on Deception Island, South Shetlands

68

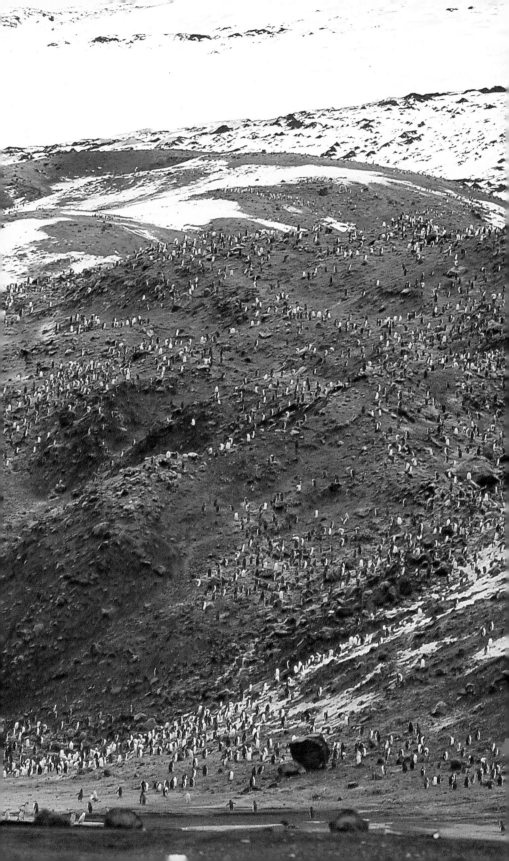

ADELIE PENGUIN

Pygoscelis adeliae
Catarrhactes adeliae
(Hombron and Jacquinot, 1841)

French: Manchot Adélie
German: Adeliepinguin
Spanish: Pingüino de Adelia
Norwegian: Adeliepingvin
Flemish: Adeliepinguïn

Description. This species was first described by naturalists exploring the austral seas aboard Jules Sébastien Dumont d'Urville's ships, the *Astrolabe* and *Zélée.* This French explorer landed on the archipelago of Pointe Geologie on January 19, 1840. He claimed these deserted islands in the name of the king of France and named the 120 miles of icy coastline Adélie Land in honor of his wife, Adèle. The new penguin species discovered during this trip bears her name.

Adults: Adélies have a very classic plumage: black and white, *de rigueur.* Black feathers cover their back from the bill to the tail. The head is black all the way to the chin, except for a white ring around the eyes. The underparts are white. The feet and underside of the flippers are pinkish. The adults have an erectile occipital crest. Its appearance (shape and height) plays an important role in the Adélies' displays.

Unconventional colorations occur as well as partial or total albinism.

Immatures: Fledglings are white and blue-black with a gray-blue bill. They develop their adult plumage and the white rings around the eyes only after the second-year molt.

Chicks: Chicks have an ashy-gray-down plumage, except for the head,which is darker. It becomes brown and thicker when they are three weeks old. They start molting two weeks later, revealing their future plumage, except for the white chin.

Length/Weight: Adults measure approximately 30 inches (75 cm).

Their weight varies with their fasting cycles. When the male arrives at the colony, he weighs about 13.2 pounds (6 kg), and the female about 11.9 pounds (5.4 kg). After the fast that follows the molt, they weigh respectively about 7.25 and 5.95 pounds (3.3 and 2.7 kg).

Breeding. Adélies make their first attempt at breeding when they are between three and eight years old. Some breeding partners stay together year after year.

The first males arrive at the rookery in the first half of October, after trudging 18 to 60 miles (30 to 100 km) across the ice pack. They settle in rocky areas (cliffs, slopes, ledges) or on sandy beaches. Then they go about finding a nest site. Their nests are very rudimentary: a saucer-shaped hollow in the ground with pebbles lining the outer edges.

The Adélies' social behavior has been studied extensively, so there is much data available. They defend their territory quite aggressively. Their antagonistic behavior manifests in different ways: by "bill-jousting" with birds in adjacent nests, or, if the intruder is farther away, by the "bill-to-axilla" display, whereby the birds rotate their head from side to side, or by the more defensive posture called "alternate stare," whereby they arch their neck while twisting their head back and forth to show alternate sides of their face. Tucking their head under an outstretched flipper is another form of aggressive display. It is interesting to note the species' generally high stress level. Waving outstretched flippers, raising the occipital crest on the nape of the neck, and dilating the white sclera are all signs of the birds' state of anxiety.

There are numerous displays that occur during the breeding season. The male begins courting by standing on top of the little pile of pebbles collected for the nest. In full sight, he points his bill skyward, stretches his flippers horizontally, and lets out loud cracking sounds. If a female responds to his call, the two mates face each other and engage in mutual bowing.

The male then prepares the nest by spreading out the pebbles with his chest and bill, and invites the female to lie in it. Copulation follows. The new pair reinforces its bond through mutual displays, in which they begin by facing each other with their bills pointed downward and end with their bills pointed upward and flippers outstretched at a 90° angle.

They engage in the same mutual displays when they return to the nest to feed

An albino Adélie, Paulet Island, Antarctic Peninsula

their chicks or to relieve the brooding partner.

The female lays two different-sized eggs six to 10 days after she arrives at the rookery, between the beginning of November and the beginning of December. The second egg, laid three days after the first, is the smallest of the two. It weighs 4 ounces (115 g) on the average, versus 4.35 ounces (124 g) for the first one. Both eggs are incubated on the parents' feet.

The male takes the first incubation shift. The female returns about 12 days later, depending on the distance between the nest and the sea. In the event of a late breakup of the ice, and the female is unable to relieve her partner in time, the male must abandon the clutch if he is to survive. Generally, the male goes back to sea after a fast of four to six weeks. A week later, he returns to relieve the female. She stays out for a week or two and returns to finish the incubation cycle. The first egg hatches about 34 days after it was laid.

Chick-Rearing. Parents take turns guarding their chicks every day or twice every three days.

The chicks join crèches when they are three weeks old and are fed once or twice a day, depending on the colony. When the parents return from foraging, they call out loudly to their chicks and engage in displays. The chicks rush out to be fed, sometimes pestering their parent by chasing it around the colony for more food.

The chicks fledge when they are 50 to 55 days old (in late January through early February). The ice pack is now broken up, and the water is near. Although they have not finished molting, they head out to the open sea on ephemeral ice floes and bergs with one last tuft of brown down on the top of their head. They return to the site two to three years later.

Ten days after the adults leave (in mid-March), they return to the rookery to molt. They stay for about 20 days, and are all gone by early April.

Foraging. Adélies feed primarily on Antarctic krill *(Euphausia superba)*. This little crustacean migrates up and down between the surface of the water and a depth of 660 feet (200 m), according to a cycle that varies with the seasons.

Distribution varies also according to the season.

During incubation, adult Adélies go foraging for four days about 54 miles (90 km) away.

During the guard stage, they forage within 12 miles (20 km) of the rookery for about 30 hours at a time.

Only when the ice breaks are they able to feed regularly. If it doesn't break until late in the season, the chicks will be underfed because the parents are away for too long.

Diet

Signy Island   King George Island

According to Lishman, 1985   *According to Volckman, 1980*

Adélie Land

According to Ridoux and Offredo, 1989

An Adélie fledgling and adult on Petterman Island in February

Adélies perched on an ephemeral iceberg, Antarctica

Adélies' preferred foraging grounds are 33 to 49.5 feet (10 to 15 m) deep in one part and 115.5 to 148.5 feet (35 to 45 m) deep in another.

The deepest recorded dive was 577.5 feet (175 m).

Their stomach content after feeding consists of 95 percent krill and weighs between 11.4 and 16.8 ounces (325 and 480 g).

Survival. The leopard seal *(Hydrurga leptonyx)* is undoubtedly the Adélies' main predator. Adults are particularly vulnerable to them on the shoreline. Leopard seals patrol the beaches at high speeds of 6.6 to 7.8 miles per hour (11 to 13 km/h), waiting for a group of Adélies to return from the open sea. As soon as they spot them, they dive and emerge with a penguin locked in their jaws, shaking it violently. It takes them 4 to 7 minutes to swallow their prey.

Leopard seals also attack fledglings as they leave the colony, using a slightly different hunting technique: they dive farther away from the young penguin swimming on the surface and burst out of the water, snatching the bird ferociously.

During fledging, leopard seals don't prey on adults, because they require a greater expenditure of energy. The floating skins left behind by the leopard seals are preyed upon avidly by skuas *(Catharacta maccormicki)* and giant petrels *(Macronectes giganteus).* Leopard seals are responsible for the death of up to 1.4 percent of the colony's adult population.

Skuas and sheathbills *(Chionis alba)* steal eggs and sometimes young chicks.

Adélies start nesting at the beginning of the austral summer, so their clutches are exposed to the elements. Many nests are destroyed by snowdrifts.

The combination of predators and harsh weather conditions destroys 45 to 70 percent of all eggs and chicks.

If the ice breaks late in the season, the adults are unable to return in time to

relieve their mate. Many chicks die because the guarding parent is forced to abandon the clutch if it is to survive.

Distribution. Adélies and emperors are the only *Spheniscidae* to breed on the Antarctic continent.

They are distributed all around the continent and on neighboring islands, such as South Shetlands, South Orkneys, Balleny, Bouvet, and so forth. They are rarely seen beyond the Antarctic Convergence.

Adélies have been spotted twice in the Falkland Islands. Single birds have been seen in New Zealand and Tasmania, and on Heard, Macquarie, and Kerguelen Islands.

Population. The breeding population was estimated in 1991 at more than 2.5 million pairs, making Adélies the second-largest penguin species in Antarctica.

The largest colonies are located on Cape Adare (Ross Sea), with 272,338 pairs; Vestfold Hills (MacRobertson Land), with 196,592 pairs; Cape Crozier (Ross Sea), with 136,249 pairs; Possession Island (Ross Sea), with 142,483 pairs; Rauer Island (Queen Elizabeth Land), with 103,916 pairs; Hope Bay (Antarctic Peninsula), with 123,850 pairs; and Paulet Island (Weddell Sea), with 60,000 pairs.

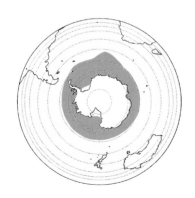

GENTOO PENGUIN

Pygoscelis papua
Aptenodytes papua
(Forster, 1781)

French: Manchot papou
German: Eselspinguin
Spanish: Pinguin de pico rojo, juanito
Norwegian: Boylepingvin
Flemish: Ezelspinguïn

The accuracy of the gentoo's scientific name *papua* has been a much-debated topic. Sonnerat mistakenly gave this name to the species during his travels to New Guinea in 1776. Forster, misled by his error, concluded that the word meant "frizzy" in Malay.

The two following subspecies are described because of their biometrical differences: *P. papua,* from the subantarctic islands, and *P. papua Ellsworthii,* from the Antarctic Peninsula and neighboring archipelagos (South Sandwich, South Orkney, South Shetland Islands).

Description. *Adults:* Gentoos are the most colorful *Pygoscelis* species. They have a standard plumage—a black back and white underparts—with white speckles sprinkled over the head and above the bill. A white band runs across the top of the head, from one eye to the other, forming a white triangular patch above each eye. The eyes are surrounded with a ring of white feathers. The bill is bright orange. The feet are pinkish orange. The underside of the flippers is pinkish white. *Immatures:* Immatures have the same plumage as adults, but the white triangular patches above the eyes are less distinct. The chin and neck are gray instead of black. The bill and feet are a paler orange. *Chicks:* Chicks are silvery gray when they hatch. A week later, the underparts from the chin down are white, the back and flippers are ashy gray, the bill is yellow-orange, and the feet are off-white.

Length/Weight: Adult gentoos measure about 30.4 inches (76 cm) in length. There is much variation in their morphology. Their length and weight increase as the latitude decreases, and vice versa.

The largest birds live in subantarctic regions, and the smallest in the islands near Antarctica. (The birds from the Kerguelen Islands are the only exception to the rule.) Gentoos living in the Morbihan Gulf (a closed bay) weigh 10.1 pounds (4.6 kg) on the average, whereas those living on Ratmanoff Beach (on the open ocean) weigh 12.5 pounds (5.7 kg) on the average. According to Bost and Jouventin, these considerable ecological variations are linked to the differences in the sites, regardless of their proximity.

The average weight of adults before molting (not including those from the Kerguelen Islands) varies from 11.45 pounds (5.2 kg) (South Orkneys) to 14.75 pounds (6.7 kg) (Crozet Islands).

Breeding. The gentoos' breeding biology varies according to the colony's location and the year. Average water temperature is an important parameter. Sites are located in two zones: the subantarctic islands, where average annual temperatures range between 39.2° and 44.6° F (4° and 7° C), and the islands near the Antarctic Convergence, where they range between 30.2°

and 35.6° F (-1° and 2° C). Temperature variations have a direct impact on the timing and synchronization of egg laying within a certain zone. (Falkland Island colonies are exceptions to the rule.)

Egg laying begins in early June on Marion Island and not until early December on the Antarctic Peninsula. Egg-laying periods in the subantarctic zones (Crozet, Marion) extend over a long period (135 to 154 days), whereas on the Antarctic Peninsula and South Shetlands, the cycle is shorter (16 to 28 days).

The longer egg-laying season enables gentoos on Crozet Island to lay a replacement clutch in the event that the first one is lost. This is not possible farther south.

The size of gentoo colonies varies greatly, from a few pairs to several thousand. Their density varies according to the latitude: the average distance between each nest is 3.3 feet (1 m) on the Antarctic Peninsula and 6.6 feet (2 m) on Crozet Island.

The materials used to build the nest vary with the site: twigs and seaweed in the subantarctic islands, and pebbles on the Antarctic Peninsula and neighboring islands. Unlike other *Pygoscelis,* gentoos nest only in snow- and ice-free areas.

Two gentoo chicks begging for food

A very young chick still bears a diamond-shaped marking at the tip of its bill.

The male is responsible for gathering the materials. He brings them back to his mate, who incorporates them in their rudimentary nest. Sometimes he snatches a twig here, a cormorant feather there, from a neighbor. Then a fight ensues with pecks and flailing flippers.

An entire colony has been known to relocate a few hundred yards away from the previous year's site, as has been the case in South Georgia and the Falkland Islands. The old site, which is trampled upon and covered with feces, is abandoned in favor of a greener site.

Gentoos are the shyest of all penguins. They defend their nest by pointing their bill downward and backing off, which is not very effective in intimidating thieves, such as skuas.

People who visit gentoo colonies should be aware that any substantial disturbance to the colony could jeopardize the clutch by making it more vulnerable to predators.

Mates are loyal to each other and come together year after year.

It is hard to pinpoint the first arrival date because the species is sedentary, especially in the subantarctic islands. The colonies located farther south disperse, but they don't actually migrate, as do Adélies.

The male secures a nest site and tries to attract the female by calling out with his bill pointed skyward. Gentoos have a very simple breeding behavior. They bow to each other, pointing their bill toward the nest, and engage in ecstatic display. Then the female lays two same-size eggs within a three-day interval.

Both partners takes turns incubating for a total of 35 days (on the average).

Chick-Rearing. After hatching, the chicks are guarded by one of the parents for 25 days, and then they join other chicks in a crèche. The parents take turns feeding their young. The chick from the first egg, who has a head start on the second one, now outrivals it by taking most of the food. It is stronger and able to push its sibling away. The second chick rarely survives. As soon as the surviving chick

A skua trying to steal an egg in a gentoo colony in the Falkland Islands

leaves the nest, the parents are able to return to sea together.

Gentoos grow slower than any other penguin species.

Chicks fledge when they are 80 days old and stay near the colony.

Foraging. The gentoo's diet varies considerably from colony to colony. The type and size of the prey change with the site, and, within the same colony, with the season and the age of the bird. Research conducted over a number of years shows that the average diet within a site also varies according to the availability of the prey.

On Crozet Island, *Euphausia valentinei* is the favorite prey. On Marion Island, the fish/crustacean ratio varies according to the season, with 82 percent crustaceans (mainly *Nauticaris marionis*) in March and 79 percent fish (*Notothenia squamifrons*) in December.

On the Antarctic Peninsula, the diet consists of crustaceans (*Euphausia superba, Parathemisto gaudichaudii*) supplemented with more fish (*Pleura-*

gramma antarcticum) than in the diet of neighboring *Pygoscelis*.

Diet

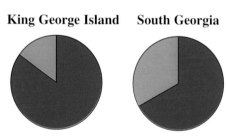

King George Island **South Georgia**

According to Volkman, 1980   *According to Croxall and Prince, 1980*

Marion Island

According to Adams and Wilson, 1987

The size of the prey depends on the species, and can range from 0.4 to 5.2 inches (10 to 130 mm) long.

Dive depths increase throughout the day, with a maximum recorded depth of 515 feet (156 m) around midday.

During the breeding season, gentoos stay within 18 miles (30 km) of the colony. They forage daily right along the shores. Because they waste little time reaching fishing grounds, they have more time to feed. They travel at an average speed of 2.7 miles per hour (4.5 km).

Survival. Brooding adults are not very aggressive in protecting their clutch or their young. Even if they do squawk, they back off when skuas attack.

The Dominican gull *(Larus dominicanus)* and striated caracara *(Phalcoboenus striatus)* steal eggs, also. They attack mainly nests on the outer edges of the colony. At sea, gentoos are preyed upon by killer whales *(Orcinus orca)* and leopard seals *(Hydrurga leptonyx)*. In some colonies in the Falkland Islands, austral sea lions *(Otaria byronia)* are also a threat. They chase gentoos right up onto the beach.

Distribution. Gentoos are spread out over a large territory. Their breeding colonies are located between 46° and 65° south latitude.

Many colonies are found on islands off the Antarctic Peninsula and in the South Shetland Islands.

Gentoos live in the Falklands, and on Kerguelen, Marion, Macquarie, Heard,

Prince Edward, Crozet, South Orkney, and South Sandwich Islands.

Population. The gentoo population is much smaller than that of other species, in spite of their wide distribution. There are between 250,000 and 300,000 breeding pairs. These figures seem to be relatively stable.

Most of the breeding population is located in the Falklands (110,000 to 120,000 pairs), on the Kerguelen Islands (30,000 to 40,000 pairs), and in South Georgia (50,000 pairs).

Some rookeries have suffered a serious decline due to the proximity of scientific bases, the exploitation of penguin oil, and commercial egging. Penguins are disturbed easily and may abandon their nests. Interference should be avoided at all costs, especially during the incubation and guarding stages.

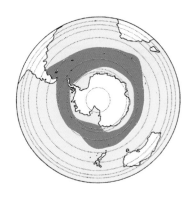

Gentoos using whale bones as shelter, Port Lokroy, Antarctic Peninsula

CHINSTRAP PENGUIN
Pygoscelis antarctica
Aptenodytes antarctica

(Forster, 1781)
Also called: Bearded penguin, stone cracker
French: Manchot à jugulaire
German: Zügelpinguin
Spanish: Pinguin de collar, pinguin de barbijo
Norwegian: Ringpingvin
Flemish: Stormbandpinguin, kinband-pinguïn

Description. *Adults:* Although the chinstrap sports the same black-and-white plumage as other species, it is without a doubt the most elegant of all, with a jet-black band running across its pure-white chin, like the strap of a helmet. It has a narrow head and bill. Its red irises stand out on its white face. Its eyes and pink feet are the only touch of color.

Immatures: Fledglings have the same plumage as adults, although the chinstrap is not very visible on their grayish face. They acquire their full adult plumage at 14 months.

Chicks: The newborn chick is covered with light-gray down. Twenty days later, it develops a new coat with a silvery-gray back and white underparts.

Length/Weight: Adults range from 28.4 to 30.4 inches (71 to 76 cm) in length, and 8.6 to 11.6 pounds (3.9 to 5.3 kg) in weight, depending on the gender and the season.

Breeding. The males arrive at the rookery from late October to early November. The females get there five days or so after the arrival of the first males. Chinstraps often share breeding sites with other penguin species, such as gentoos (*P. papua*) and Adélies (*P. adeliae*), or with imperial cormorants (*Phalacro-*

corax albiventer). They are a gregarious species. Their colonies can be very large, extending over slopes inland many hundreds of yards. Distances between nests average 24 inches (60 cm).

Fidelity among mates is strong, so chinstraps generally pair up with the same mate from one year to the next.

They usually return to the previous year's nest (82 percent of the time in Admiralty Bay). New breeders find a rocky hollow, and they keep adding rocks and bones during the entire breeding cycle.

Chinstraps are not as hardworking or creative as other *Pygoscelis* species, as

A chinstrap tucked in the snow on Thulé Island

82

An adult chinstrap adding more rocks to the nest, even though its chick is grown

reflected in the simplicity of their nests, although they are more pugnacious. There has been no extensive research into their breeding behavior, but the many behavioral studies conducted on the *Pygoscelis adeliae* can be said to apply to this species.

Two weeks after copulation, from late November to early December, the female lays two eggs, three days apart. A third egg may be laid three days after the second egg if the first one becomes lost.

Incubation generally lasts 37 days. The female is responsible for the first six days; then both partners take turns incubating the eggs with more or less regularity.

Chick-Rearing. During the first two weeks, the chicks are fed twice daily. Feedings become scarcer as they grow older. The interval between feedings varies, depending on the distance between the colony and the foraging grounds. Breeders on Elephant Island travel 9 to 21 miles (15 to 35 km) to reach schools of krill; those on Signy Island, 36 miles (60 km). The amount of food brought back increases as the chicks grow older. If the clutch is reduced to one chick, the surviving bird grows much faster.

The chicks molt in early February and fledge in mid-March at the latest.

The adults molt from mid-February to mid-March, depending on the site. It takes 13 days to renew their plumage.

Foraging. Chinstraps feed mainly on Antarctic krill (*Euphausia superba*): this crustacean accounts for 98 to 100 percent

83

of their diet. In certain areas, such as King George and Signy Islands, their diet is supplemented with small fish (*Pleuragramma antarcticum, Trematomus eulepidotus*) and amphipods (*Hyperia macrocephala, Themisto gaudichaudii*). Preys measure 0.6 to 2.4 inches (15 to 60 mm). The weight of breeding adults' stomach content ranges from 6.5 to 18.4 ounces (185 to 527 g), on Elephant Island, depending on the age of the chicks.

Chinstraps generally dive within 132 feet (40 m) of the surface (in 90 percent of the measurements recorded), and their

Diet

Signy Island

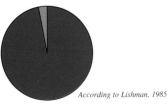

According to Lishman, 1985

maximum recorded dive is 231 feet (70 m). The average foraging dive duration is 1 minute and 50 seconds.

The feeding hours fluctuate according to the location. Chinstraps in the vicinity of Signy Island seem to feed mostly at night (shallow dives), whereas those from King George Island feed only during the day.

Survival. Leopard seals (*Hydrurga leptonyx*) are undoubtedly chinstraps' main predator. There are many throughout the region, and they attack single birds along the coastline, regardless of the penguins' age. Sheathbills (*Chionis alba*) snatch many eggs, and skuas (*Catharacta sp.*) prey upon chicks.

Distribution. The range of the chinstrap is much larger than that of the Adélie. Chinstraps are found mostly along the Scotia Arc on archipelagos, such as the South Shetlands, South Orkneys, and South Sandwich Islands, where 75 percent of the population live. Smaller colonies have settled on the southeast shores of South Georgia, on Bouvet and Balleny Islands, and on the islands west of the Antarctic Peninsula. A few couples breed on the Antarctic continent.

They have also been spotted in the Falklands, in Tasmania, on Macquarie, Marion, and Gough Islands, and in Adélie Land. Adults migrate north in early April, deserting their Antarctica Peninsula rookeries. Immatures wander far away, following schools of krill.

Population. The chinstrap breeding population is estimated at approximately 7.5 million pairs and appears to be growing in most colonies. Big krill-eaters, chinstraps are benefiting from an increase in the krill population due to the decrease in the population of whales.

The largest colonies are located in the Sandwich Islands, mainly on Zavodovski Island, with a total of 5 million breeding pairs, and in the South Shetlands, with 480,000 breeding pairs on King George Island, 295,000 on Low Island, and 70,000 on Deception Island.

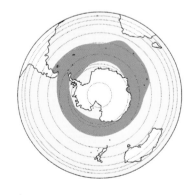

An adult chinstrap feeding a chick

85

Genus *Eudyptula*

Eudyptula minor, commonly known as little penguin or blue penguin, is the only species in this genus. The little penguin is indigenous to southern Australia and New Zealand. Its morphology is different from that of other penguin species, and it is nocturnal. Regarded as the most primitive species on the evolutionary scale, little penguins are reminiscent of their petrel and puffin ancestors. The genus name means "good little diver" in Greek.

Among the subspecies, the white-flippered penguin (*E. minor albosignata*) is often considered a separate species altogether. Little penguins, like small *Procellariformes* and *Spheniscus* penguins, nest in burrows protected from the sun and predators.

A breeding pair of little penguins nests in a rock crevice on Whale Island.

LITTLE PENGUIN

Eudyptula minor
Aptenodytes minor
(Forster, 1781)

Also called: Little blue penguin, fairy
penguin, blue penguin
French: Petit manchot bleu
German: Zwergpinguin
Norwegian: Dvergpingvin
Flemish: Dwergpinguïn
Maori: Korara
Aborigine: Choolia, indala, munuwar

The species is divided into different sub-
species, according to their location, size,
and color:
E. m. minor (South Australia)
E. m. iredalei (north of North Island,
New Zealand)
E. m. variabilis (south of North Island,
New Zealand)
E. m. albosignata (east of South Island,
New Zealand)
E. m. chathamensis (Chatham Island)
E. m. novaehollandiae (Phillip Island)

Description. *Adults:* The back, flippers
(dorsally), and top of the head are varying shades of indigo blue, depending on
the subspecies. *E. m. minor* is the darkest
of all. *E. m. albosignata* is the lightest,
and it is recognizable by the white mar-
gins on the leading and trailing edges of
its flippers, and by another white band,
more or less visible, that runs across the
flippers one-third up from the tip. The
rest of the body (underparts, chin, underside of flippers) is white.
Immatures: Fledglings have the same
plumage as that of adults, but it is brighter.
Chicks: Newly hatched chicks are covered in grayish-brown down, which is
replaced a week later by chocolate-brown
down on the back and light-gray down on
the belly. Chicks begin to develop adult
plumage when they are one month old.
Length/Weight: This is the smallest of
all penguin species. The adults are 16.4

to 18 inches (41 to 45 cm) long, like
Brünnich's guillemot (*Alca lomvia*), of
the auk family, which measures an average of 17.2 inches (43 cm).

There are a few distinctions between
the genders, notably the size and shape of
the bill: the male's bill is 15 percent
thicker and 6 percent longer than the
female's. The males also seem to be
more robust. The average weight of the
little penguin is 2.2 pounds (1 kg), but it
fluctuates with the seasons and according
to the penguin's age and gender.

Daily Rhythm: This species' daily
rhythm is unique. Little penguins are
nocturnal on land. They return from the
sea only at night, with 95 percent of the
colony's birds coming ashore within a
period of two hours.

This year-round behavior can be explained in three ways. First, it can be seen
as a behavioral adaptation to a thermoreg-
ulatory problem: well protected against the
cold waters, the little penguin likes to
avoid the heat of the day. This kind of
behavior is common also among fur seals,
such as *A. galapagoensis*. Second, it can be
explained by the absence of nocturnal land
predators. And third, it can be accounted
for by looking at the behavior of its prey:
krill and cephalopods move to the surface
of the sea at dusk, which allows penguins
to complete their foraging at shallow
depths before returning to land.

Breeding. The breeding season begins in
late March on Penguin Island and in late
April through early May on Phillip Island.

Little penguins use two types of nest sites, depending on the location: a burrow or a sea cave. Their breeding behavior varies accordingly.

The males return to their colonies to prepare a nest site, over which they often have to fight. Once they claim a site, they dig the burrow with their feet in the sand dune 24 to 32 inches (60 to 80 cm) deep, preferably under a clump of tussock grass because of the stabilizing effect of its roots on the substratum. The burrow consists of a tunnel and a nesting chamber, or bowl. Some penguins nest in puffin burrows.

Once the males establish their territory, they stand at the entrance of their burrow and try to attract a mate through a series of calls while engaging in ecstatic display. On a rocky site, males gather together in calling clubs in central, non-breeding areas.

Once the pair forms, the mates set out to find a favorable nesting site in a rock crevice. The same breeding pairs form year after year, and often return to the same nest site.

The distance between nests is approximately 6.6 feet (2 m) all around. Both mates actively defend their territory. Little penguins ward off intruders by means of an extensive array of antagonistic behaviors, ranging from intimidation to overt aggression that sometimes results in severe wounds. These behaviors are always accompanied by vocalizations that vary according to the situation, from low-pitched growls to a series of loud squeals.

Between September and October, the female lays two white eggs in the nest

lined with leaves deep in the burrow, 68 hours apart. The eggs weigh an average of 1.85 ounces (53 g).

Incubation lasts approximately 36 days (33 to 45). The parents take turns on the clutch every two to three days.

Chick-Rearing. Chicks stay in the nest 56 days (48 to 59) after hatching. They are fed daily by one parent during the first weeks, then by both. They grow quickly and weigh 2.4 pounds (1.1 kg) at fledging.

The parents guard the chicks for three weeks, until they can regulate their body temperature through their layer of down. Then they are left in the nest unguarded. Two weeks later, at dusk, the chicks wait for their ration of food outside their burrow. Chicks call out to their parents with a peeping or a hissing sound.

Once the breeding cycle is over, the parents molt for two to three weeks. They lose 50 percent of their weight, but they gain it back as soon as they return to sea to feed.

Foraging. The little penguins' diet varies according to their location, the season, and the migration of shoaling fish and invertebrates. Little penguins are opportunistic and take advantage of the most abundant prey.

Fish predominates their diet (75 to 98 percent). On the coast of Victoria, the main prey are *Engraulis australis* (from February to June) and *Sardinops neopilchardus* (from August to November), supplemented by other fish species, such as *Clupeides sp.,* and cephalopods (*Loliolus noctiluca, Sepioteuthis australis, etc.),* when the preferred prey is not as abundant.

Their diet is steadier on Penguin Island (southwestern Australia), where *Hyperlophus vittatus* are present year round. In the fall and winter, their diet is supplemented with *Sardinops neopilchardus* and *Hyporhamphus melanochir,* and in the spring and summer, with *Spratelloides robustus.*

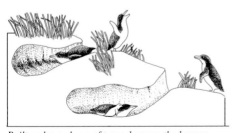

Built under a clump of tussock grass, the burrow consists of a tunnel and a nesting chamber.

Diet

Philip Island (Australia)

According to Van Heezik, 1900

South of New Zealand, on Codfish Island, their diet consists mainly of *Auchenoceros punctatus* and *Pseudophycis bachus,* with a regular supplement of cephalopods, *Nototodarus sloanii.*

In the waters south of Tasmania, krill is also an important part of their diet.

Little penguins forage alone or in small groups of six, and they use different techniques to capture their shoaling prey. They sometimes herd a shoal of little fish into a shallow bay, as do some dolphins, and dive through the middle. The cycle is repeated several times before the fish have a chance to disperse. They also may close in on the shoal quickly and dart into it at a high speed of 4.5 miles per hour (7.5 km/h), thus dispersing the prey. They capture the prey as they dive through the middle of the shoal and also chase isolated prey after they disperse.

Little penguins eat their prey underwater. Their average diving depth is 99 feet (30 m). The maximum depth recorded is 227 feet (69 m).

Prey rarely measure more than 2 inches (50 mm).

Little penguins each consume approximately 198 pounds (90 kg) of food every year.

Survival. Blue-tongued lizards, tiger snakes, skuas (*Catharacta skua*), Dominican gulls (*Larus dominicanus*), Pacific gulls (*Larus pacificus*), and sea eagles prey upon penguin eggs and chicks.

At sea, adults and immatures are prey to sea lions (*Neophoca cinerea* and *Phocarctos hookeri*), sharks, and barracudas.

Little penguins have to cope not only with natural predators but with dogs, cats, weasels, ferrets, rats, and other animals that were introduced by seafarers and settlers. These predators attack adult penguins, destroy nests, and feed on eggs and chicks.

Distribution. Little penguin colonies are scattered along the southern and eastern coasts of Australia and on the shores of New Zealand, Tasmania, and Chatham Islands.

Adults are sedentary, but, from April to August, some leave the colony for nearby waters. Sixty-day-old immatures disperse along the coasts in different directions, depending on where their colony is located. Birds from Phillip Island head west, those from Five Island point south, and those from the Gulf of Hauraki go north.

They return to their colony when they are three years old (and on rare occasions, when they are two).

Population. The Australian little penguin population is estimated at less than one million birds. Despite the many plagues that afflict the species, including human interference, the population appears to be stable, except in certain locations, such as Phillip Island, where its population has dropped considerably.

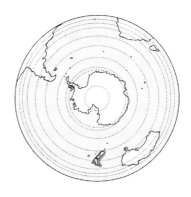

Genus *Megadyptes*

There is only one species in the *Megadyptes* genus: the yellow-eyed penguin. It is endemic to the coasts of New Zealand.

Megadyptes means "big diver."

The yellow-eyed penguin (*Megadyptes antipodes*) is recognizable by its yellow irises, as its name indicates.

With a pale-yellow band running around the back of its head from eye to eye, it is sometimes mistaken for the crested penguin that also lives along New Zealand shores.

It is the least gregarious species and hides under vegetation.

A yellow-eyed penguin molting

YELLOW-EYED PENGUIN

Megadyptes antipodes
Catarrhactes antipodes
(Hombron and Jacquinot, 1841)

French: Manchot à oeil jaune
German: Gelbaugenpinguin
Norwegian: Guloyepingvin
Flemish: Antipodenpinguïn, geeloogpin-
guïn
Maori: Takaraka

Description. *Adults:* The main characteristic of the yellow-eyed penguin's
plumage is the straw-yellow band that
runs from one corner of the bill to the
other across its yellow eyes and around
the top of the head. The yellowish cheeks
are bordered by reddish hues along the
neck and sides. The rest of the head and
chin are yellowish gray. The nape, back,
and upperside of the flippers are black.
The underparts are white. The bill is
pink, with a white border running from
the base to the middle. The feet are pink.
  The yellow-eyed penguin's territory
overlaps with the little penguins' and the
fiordlands'. These three species are very
different. The little penguin is Lilliputian
compared to the large fiordland. At sea,
the yellow headband of the yellow-eyed
penguin sets it apart from all other local
penguin species.
  Immatures: Immatures have no yellow
band crowning their head, but their eyes
are already pale yellow. Their chin is
grayish white. The yellow headband
develops when they are between 14 and
18 months old.
  Chicks: Chicks are dark brown at
hatching. They put on a lighter down
three weeks later.
  Length/Weight: Yellow-eyed penguins
measure between 22.4 and 31.2 inches
(56 and 78 cm) in length.
  Their weight fluctuates, depending on
the season. The males weigh about 18.7

pounds (8.5 kg) before molting, and 9.7
pounds (4.4 kg) after. The females lose
7.25 pounds (3.3 kg) during the molting
period, going from 16.5 pounds (7.5 kg)
to 9.25 pounds (4.2 kg). During the nesting season, the males weigh approximately 12.3 pounds (5.6 kg), and
females, 11 pounds (5 kg).

Breeding. Yellow-eyed penguins are
sedentary birds and never venture far
from their breeding grounds. Most breeding adults start settling into their nest in
late August through early September.
They are familiar with the site, because
they spend every winter night there. Pairs
form throughout the year. Some birds
find a new partner and build a fresh nest
at the end of the breeding cycle, whereas
others are faithful to their mate and to
their nest site year after year.
  As with other penguin species, the male
tries to attract a female through an ecstatic display with his bill pointed skyward
and flippers outstretched. He approaches
cautiously and stands before her with his
bill raised. She answers in the same way.
The male and female confirm their bond
by engaging in a series of mutual displays, face to face, synchronizing their
postures and calls. The calls are quieter
and more melodious than other penguins', because yellow-eyed colonies are
small and the birds are not forced to raise
their voices to be heard over the multitude of other voices.
  Yellow-eyed penguins are the least gregarious species during breeding season.

There are no more than one to five nests for every 2.5 acres (1 hectare).

They don't dig burrows but rather use the coastal vegetation to build nests with leaves, twigs, and branches, and to protect themselves against the heat of the sun. The newly formed pair searches for a suitable nesting site. The number of nests per acre is directly proportional to the quality (density and height) of the plants and shrubs present. Some nests are located at the top of 300-foot (90-m) cliffs. The pair defends their territory with aggressive displays and calls. The female lays the clutch in late September through early October.

Females are mature when they are two years old. They generally lay only one egg during the first breeding season. The following year, they lay two eggs, each weighing an average of 4.55 ounces (130 g).

Incubation lasts 39 to 51 days. Both the male and the female share incubation duties equally, relieving their partner every other day.

Chick-Rearing. Young chicks are blind and remain between their parents' feet as they were before they hatched.

Twenty days later, they trade their thick down for a shorter down and begin venturing outside the nest.

After a six-week guarding stage, they are left alone, while their parents go foraging, until they return to feed them in the late afternoon.

The success rate of breeding is estimated at 1.3 chicks per breeding pair, and only 0.50 in areas with high populations of introduced predators.

Breeding adults molt after the breeding season, generally between February and March. The molt lasts 24 days. Immatures and nonbreeding adults renew their plumage during the chick-rearing stage.

Foraging. Yellow-eyed penguins are ichthyophagous. Their diet consists of 97 to 98 percent fish, supplemented by a few cephalopods. However, immatures consume a greater amount of squid.

Their prey varies according to the season and the locality. Twenty-six taxons have been identified in the yellow-eyed's foraging range.

Breeding birds from the Otago Peninsula feed on such fish as *Pseudophycis bachus, Hemerocoetes monopterygius,* and *Parapercis colias,* and such cephalopods as *Nototodarus sloanii* and *Octopus maorum.* During the winter months, they also eat species like *Auchenoceros punctatus.*

Diet

South Island, New Zealand

According to Van Heezik, 1990

Their prey measure between 0.8 and 12.8 inches (20 and 320 mm). The stomach content of an adult (approximately 11.9 ounces) is about 6 percent of its entire weight.

Breeding adults forage 4.2 to 7.8 miles (7 to 13 km) off the coast (Otago Peninsula), and dive 102 to 115 feet (31 to 35 m) under the surface, with a maximum recorded depth of 185 feet (56 m). Some penguins have been found drowned in fishing nets at a depth of 330 feet (100 m).

Survival. The leopard seal (*Hydrurga leptonyx*), though few in number, preys occasionally on adults at sea. The New Zealand sea lion (*Phocarctos hookeri*) is not a primary predator, but, in places like Campbell Island, its presence alters the penguins' behavior: they avoid the beaches where these sea lions lie about, and head out to sea when they are patrolling nearby. The sea lion grabs the penguin at sea and carries it away from the shore, thrashing it from side to side before tearing it to pieces. Yet elsewhere, such as on Enderby Island, penguins waddle a few feet away from sea lions without being attacked. The barracuda (*Thyrsites atun*) is another potential predator and is known to inflict serious wounds on the birds.

However, human encroachment is by far the greatest threat to yellow-eyed penguins. The expansion of cattle-grazing lands has led to the destruction of the species' natural biotopes. Without ade-

quate foliage, the chicks are more sensitive to weather conditions. Even worse has been the introduction of dogs, cats, and ferrets, because of the proximity of farms to breeding grounds. These predators attack eggs and young chicks, potentially destroying up to 90 percent of a colony's young.

Distribution. Indigenous to New Zealand, most of the yellow-eyed penguin population nests on the shores of the Otago Peninsula and on the east coast of South Island. Other groups breed on

South Island's southeast coast, on Stewart Island, and as far as Auckland and Campbell Islands.

Adults stay near the breeding grounds year round, whereas immatures disperse to the north.

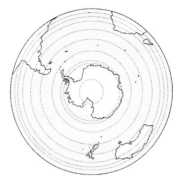

Population. There are an estimated 7,000 yellow-eyed penguins. The species has suffered a 75 percent decline in 40 years as a result of various forms of human interference. The population is not renewing itself due to the genetic isolation of certain colonies and a sharp drop in the rate of reproduction—especially on South Island of New Zealand.

A yellow-eyed pair nesting under vegetation

Genus *Spheniscus*

Encamped on subantarctic outposts, *Spheniscus* species were introduced to European naturalists in the beginning of the 16th century.

The four species—magellanic, African, Humboldt, and Galápagos penguins—were mistaken for *Alcidae* and consequently called penguins. Seamen were familiar with the great auk (*Alca impennes*), an apterous *Alcidae* from the arctic regions that was similar in size and appearance to the *Spheniscus* penguin.

Spheniscus is a Greek word meaning "wedge shaped," referring to the triangular shape of the penguin's flippers. *Spheniformes* and *Spheniscidae* have the same origin.

The three species have a similar black-and-white plumage. The only touch of color is a pink, fleshy patch at the base of the bill. *Spheniscus* are recognizable by the black, inverted-horseshoe-shaped band that surrounds their white underparts. Their powerful hooked bill is blue-gray.

They live in temperate, and sometimes warm, climates, nesting in burrows or rock caves to protect their offspring from the heat of the austral sun and from predators.

Chicks sheltered in their burrows don't feel the need for group protection, so they rarely gather in crèches. Rather, they stay near the nest until they fledge.

Magellanic penguins taking turns braying

MAGELLANIC PENGUIN

Spheniscus magellanicus
Aptenodytes magellanicus
(Forster, 1781)

Also called: Magellan penguin, jackass penguin
French: Manchot de Magellan
German: Magellanpinguin
Spanish: Pingüinos de Magallanes, pajaro Niño, pajaro manco, pingüino del sur
Norwegian: Magellanpingvin
Flemish: Magelhaenpinguin
Fuegian: Choncha

Description. Antonio Pigafetta, an Italian who chronicled Ferdinand Magellan's expedition to the mouth of the Rio de la Plata in late December of 1519, was the first to describe the species, which scientists later named after the great explorer. His account, written in a journal, was circulated privately at first and then published in Paris in a French translation in about 1525. Pigafetta called the penguins encountered on the expedition geese, because geese were large, fat, and edible, as were penguins.

Adults: The plumage of the megellanic penguin is black and white with a pink, fleshy patch between the eyes above the bluish-gray bill. The black-and-white markings are similar to other *Spheniscus* species. The white underparts are surrounded by an oval black band. A second black band runs across the base of the throat. A white band runs from the top of the bill above the eyes down and around to join across the throat, delineating the two black cheeks. The magellanic is sometimes mistaken for the Humboldt penguin (*Spheniscus humboldti*) in the northern part of its area of distribution on the Peruvian coast. The difference is that the *S. humboldti* has a white band that runs from the forehead over the eyes down across the chin joining the white

breast band, whereas the *S. magellanicus* has a black band separating its white throat from its white breast.

Immatures: Fledglings have a pearl-gray body with white underparts. The top of their head is gray and the cheeks, white. The typical black-and-white markings appear at the age of two.

Chicks: Chicks are dark gray when they hatch, but their underparts soon turn white.

Length/Weight: Magellanics measure about 28.4 inches (71 cm). The male's flippers are about 7.8 inches (19.5 cm) long, and the female's, 7.4 inches (18.6 cm).

Adult males weigh 6.4 pounds (2.9 kg) after molting and 10.5 pounds (4.8 kg) before. Females weigh between 5.9 pounds (2.7 kg) and 9 pounds (4.1 kg), depending on the season.

Breeding. Magellanics nest in burrows that they dig in flat areas. The burrows can be shallow or deep, depending on the location. The nest consists of a nesting chamber located above the tunnel floor. Some pairs nest in shallow bowls, exposing their chicks to weather conditions and increased predation from volant animals.

Heavy rain occasionally seeps into the burrows, and the penguins must clean out the mud by ejecting it with their feet.

In the Falkland Islands, the burrows are dug in sand or peat, often under clumps of tussock grass (*Poa flabellata*). The chicks can venture out of the nest without having to fear a predator attack as long as they stay under the large leaves of neighboring bushes. The nest is made of plant debris. People must be extremely careful when moving about a magellanic colony with no vegetation. The roofs of the burrows are fragile and can collapse easily under the weight of a human body. Fidelity to the nest is generally high, and pairs breed in the same burrow year after year. Magellanic colonies are scattered along the coast. At Punta Tombo (Argentina), the penguins don't always dig burrows but make their nests in the cool shade under a plant canopy.

The males arrive at the rookery in early September, and the females four to five days after the first males. In the Falklands, the breeding season is delayed two to three weeks toward the end of the year.

The magellanic's call sounds like a donkey's bray. The males advertise their nest by standing at the entrance to the burrow and braying with their bill pointed skyward and their flippers open wide. The calling is most intense in the late afternoon and late at night.

If any bird accidentally ventures into a burrow occupied by a newly formed pair, it is likely to reemerge bloodied and sometimes seriously wounded.

The eggs are laid a month after copulation, between October 5 and 25 in Argentina, depending on the year. The female lays two identical eggs (between 3.5 and 5.25 ounces), four to five days apart. She takes the first incubation shift after the second egg is laid. The male takes over 15 days later and incubates the clutch for 17 days or so. Then the birds

An adult with its two chicks basking in the January sun in front of their burrow, Falkland Islands

An austral sea lion chases a magellanic penguin on a beach in the Falkland Islands.

relieve each other every four days until hatching. Incubation lasts a total of 38 to 42 days, and 45 days in the Falklands. The eggs hatch within two days of each other, around mid-November.

Chick-Rearing. In Argentina, the parents alternate guarding duties and foraging trips every three to five days, for 60 hours or so, during the first 10 days after hatching. Foraging trips get longer as the days go by (120 hours on the average), which enables the parents to bring back more food for their growing chicks. In the Falklands, foraging runs during the chick-rearing stage last an average of 22.8 hours and occur within 30 miles (50 km) of the colony.

When an intruder approaches, the guarding parent stands in front of the chicks, hiding them. Magellanics defend their offspring by slightly raising their neck, and, because of their close-range monocular vision, they observe the trespasser with the left and then the right eye, alternately. They occasionally make a hissing sound.

It is interesting to compare the behavior of the chicks in the two largest magellanic colonies, in Punta Tombo and the Falkland Islands. Chicks from the Argentine colony

gather in crèches when they are 20 to 23 days old and stay there until they fledge, whereas those from the British archipelago remain in or around the burrow.

All immatures, regardless of their colony, fledge in early February. Adults leave the rookery in February and March after molting.

Foraging. Magellanics are spread out over a large territory, on the Atlantic and Pacific coasts. Their diet obviously varies with the location. It also varies with the seasons.

In the Falkland Islands, during the chick-feeding stage, the parents head out to sea in groups before dawn (4 a.m.) and return in the early evening (6 p.m.). Magellanics, as with their *Spheniscus* cousins, don't often porpoise but alternate 20-second dives with 20-second surface swimming. Their underwater speed is 4.5 miles per hour (7.6 km/h). They fish at an average depth of 198 feet (60 m). The maximum dive depth ever recorded was 297 feet (90 m).

Their prey measure between 1 and 6.4 inches (2.5 and 16 cm).

The weight of their stomach content varies also with the location and the season. For example, the average on New

Island (Falklands) is 2.5 ounces (72.8 g) during incubation and 13.3 ounces (380 g) during chick-feeding. Their stomach-content weight on the Argentine coast during chick-feeding is about 24 ounces (686 g).

Chick-rearing adults from the coasts of South America feed on pelagic shoaling species. Their main prey in the Pacific are *Engraulis ringens, Sprattus fuegensis,* and *Ramnogaster arcuata*, and in the Atlantic, *Engraulis anchoita, Merluccius hubbdi,* and *Austroatherina smitta.*

In the Falkland Islands, small cephalopods *(Cranchiid* and *Gonatid)* predominate the diet during incubation. During chick-rearing, fish (mostly *Notonidae)* become the

Diet

New Island, Falkland Islands

According to Thompson, 1989

bulk of the diet, supplemented by crustaceans *(Munidae sp.)* in varying proportions, depending on the site.

Survival. In the Falkland Islands, especially on the east coast of East Falkland, austral sea lions *(Otaria byronia)* prey upon adult magellanics. These sea lions patrol some 30 feet off the beach, diving underwater for long periods of time until they spot a penguin at the water's edge. Suddenly a sea lion will appear on the sandy beach, carried in by a powerful breaker. It chases the penguin, often grabbing it by the head, and carries it out to sea. It doesn't eat the ripped-off head and skin, to the delight of giant petrels *(Macronectes giganteus)* and skuas *(Catharacta skua).*

Among the magellanics' volant predators are the efficient striated caracara *(Phalcoboenus australis)*, which likes to feed on chick heads and sick adults; the Turkish vulture *(Cathartes aura)*, which ventures into unguarded burrows; and the Dominican gull *(Larus dominicanus)*, which steals penguin eggs skillfully in both breeding sites.

Distribution. Megellanics inhabit several thousand miles of South American coastline on the Pacific and the Atlantic. In Chile, they are found up to 37° south latitude, and in Argentina, up to 41° south latitude. The largest colonies are in Argentina (Punta Tombo) and the Falkland Islands. Magellanics also occur in the Juan Fernandez Islands. They

Volant predators are known to attack chicks outside their burrows.

A magellanic penguin emerges out of a wave near the beach.

migrate north during the winter to southern Brazil and Peru.

Stragglers have even been spotted near Rio de Janeiro, in South Georgia, Tristan da Cunha, and New Zealand, and on Phillip Island in Australia. Magellanics also have been seen south of their breeding grounds near Palmer Station on the Antarctic Peninsula.

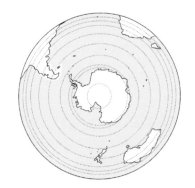

Population. It is hard to estimate the total number of magellanic penguins because of the varying densities of the colonies. Two Argentine colonies out of 21 are home to 428,500 pairs. In the Falklands, there are likely to be several thousand pairs.

AFRICAN PENGUIN

Spheniscus demersus
Aptenodytes demersa
(Linné, 1758)

Also called: Jackass penguin, blackfoot penguin
French: Manchot du Cap, manchot moyen, manchot du Cap de Bonne-Espérance
German: Brillenpinguin
Spanish: Pinguinos Africanos
Norwegian: Kappingvin
Flemish: Brilpinguïn
Afrikaners: Brilpikkewyne

Description. *Adults:* The African penguin's head is whiter than that of other *Spheniscus* species, except for the black mask that covers part of the cheeks and chin and surrounds the eyes. The eyes are also surrounded by pink skin, and the bill is black with a white transverse band one-third up from the tip. The underparts are entirely white. The black dorsal plumage ends in a black band at the base of the bill. The African penguin is also recognizable by the black, inverted-horseshoe-shaped band that runs from the feet up across the breast, delineating the white underparts. The feet are black.

Immatures: Immatures are black and white with no visible markings.

Chicks: Chicks are dark gray with whitish underparts when they hatch. A new plumage appears on the breast when they are four to five weeks old.

Length/Weight: Adults measure between 25 and 27 inches (63 and 68 cm) in length. They reach their maximum weight, about 9.4 pounds (4.3 kg), right before molting.

Breeding. African penguins are found mostly on islands and islets, although some groups have colonized large caves on the mainland. These natural shelters are inaccessible to land predators, such as black-back jackals (*Canis mesomelas*) and brown hyenas (*Hyaena brunnea*). African penguins nest in burrows to protect their offspring from the heat of the austral summer and from predators. They dig them in the guano (if it hasn't been harvested) and in the sand (at the risk of having it collapse). More and more, they are using natural cavities. When there is no malleable substratum, they simply nest in the open air. The male and female take turns digging with their flippers and feet. The nests are made of twigs, roots, and dried grass or seaweed.

African penguins breed year round, but each site has its more favorable breeding periods. There are two peak times at different locations. On the west coast, the peak is May to September, during the austral winter. Food is abundant and temperatures are moderate, making chick-rearing easier. On the east coast, the peak is November to January, during the summer. Many eggs are laid at that time.

The sexual behavior of the African penguin is very elaborate, combining all the postures observed in other penguin species. The male arrives at the breeding site, finds a burrow, and advertises his presence by calling out with an ecstatic display. The female answers the call by approaching the male and circling him.

103

And off they go, waddling one behind the other. Later, they face each other and rub bills. They will continue to rub bills during copulation. Mutual preening and face-to-face duets with raised bills reinforce their bond.

The female lays two greenish eggs, two days apart. The first egg is the largest. Incubation lasts around 38 days. The parents take turns incubating every other day. Nest relief is accomplished through discreet calls and head movements pointing toward the burrow.

Chick-Rearing. Chicks stay in or near the nest during the guarding stage. Later, they often gather in small groups of four to 11 birds to ward off aggressive adults. They shed their down after five to six weeks and put on their juvenile plumage. They fledge when they are 80 days old.

Adults molt for 20 days or so, before or after breeding.

The pre-molt feeding cycle lasts longer (63 days) if the birds are about to breed. Otherwise, it lasts only 35 days.

Foraging. The African penguin, as with other *Spheniscus*, eats mostly shoaling fish (68 percent): *Sufflogobius bibarbatus, Engraulis capensis, Sardinops ocellata, Etrumeus teres,* and *Trachurus trachurus.* It supplements its diet with crustaceans: *Squilla armata, Nyctiphares capensis, Jasus lalandii* (juvenile) and *polychetes* (11 percent).

Prey vary in size and can measure up to 12.4 inches (31 cm) in length.

Nonbreeding adults forage at least 12 miles (20 km) off the coast. Adults responsible for feeding the young forage within a 12- to 48-mile (20- to 80-km) range. Food is more abundant in the open sea, so breeding adults must travel farther as the chicks grow, in order to meet their increasing needs. They must also swim faster to keep up with the daily feeding cycle.

African penguins reach fishing grounds by alternately swimming at the surface (at an average speed of 9 miles per hour) and underwater (4.2 miles per hour). Sometimes they porpoise and exceed 7.2 miles per hour. They reach fish shoals by midday, dive 66 to 99 feet (20 to 30 m) deep, and ingest as many fish as possible. The maximum recorded exploration dive is 429 feet (130 m). Dives generally don't exceed 150 seconds. The longer dives seem to indicate that the penguin has located a good feeding area.

Survival. The biggest eater of African penguin eggs, apart from humans, is the Dominican gull (*Larus dominicanus*). This patient thief waits for the parent's slightest distraction to steal the egg. Dominican gulls sometimes work in pairs: one creates a diversion while the other steals the egg. Gulls also benefit from human interference, because the diminishing guano (see "The Exploitation of Penguins") forces the penguins to nest in shallower burrows or in the open air. Without proper shelter, their clutch is more vulnerable to predation.

The Dominican gull (*Larus dominicanus)* and other volant predators, such as the sacred ibis (*Threskiornis aethiopicus),* prey on chicks. Domesticated cats can also be added to the chick's predator list.

Adults and immatures have to contend with Cape fur seals (*Arctocephalus pusillus pusillus*) and many sharks, such as the blue shark (*Prionace glauca*) and the white shark (*Carcharodon carcharias*).

Distribution. The African penguin is the only species in Africa. It is found along the Atlantic and Indian coasts of South Africa. On the west coast, the northern limit is at latitude 24° 50' S. on Hollamsbird Island. On the east coast, in the Indian Ocean, the species breeds as far north as Algoa Bay at latitude 33° 50' S. There are 30 African penguin sites, including 27 islands.

Population. In 1992, the population was estimated at 120,000 birds. In 1930, there were more than one million. The population has suffered a 90 percent decline and is at its lowest since the turn of the century. There are many reasons for this decline, all caused by humans: egging, guano harvesting, oil spills, and overfishing prey species. The combination of all these human interferences threatens the survival of the species.

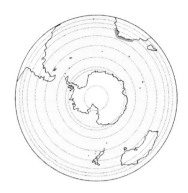

A dense group of African penguins at sunset

HUMBOLDT PENGUIN

Spheniscus humboldti
(Meyen, 1834)

Also called: Peruvian penguin
French: Manchot de Humboldt
German: Humboldtpinguin
Spanish: Pajaro Niño
Norwegian: Humboldtpingvin
Flemish: Humboldt-pinguïn
Araucan: Petranca

Description. *Adults:* The Humboldt penguin looks a great deal like its close cousin, the magellanic. A white band runs from its feet up the body and across the neck, loops over the external auditory meatus, and ends in a thin strip at the base of the bill. The underparts are white. The bill is grayish blue with a white transverse band one-third up from the tip. The bill is longer and stouter than the magellanic's.

This species has a distinctive fleshy, pink area that extends from the eyes to the mandible.

Unlike the magellanic, the Humboldt has no black band around the neck but has black speckles on its white breast. Its body is rounder than the magellanic's.

Immatures: Fledglings have a less elaborate plumage than adults. Their cheeks, chin, and neck are ashy gray, and the distinctive white bands are not yet formed.

Chicks: Chicks are covered in a grayish-brown down.

Length/Weight: Adults measure between 27 and 29 inches (67 and 72 cm) in length. Males weigh up to 10.75 pounds (4.9 kg).

Breeding. Humboldts, like other penguins of the *Spheniscus* genus, generally nest in excavated burrows in the sand or guano, and occasionally in crevices or little caves. In cooler regions, they sometimes nest in the open. They may share breeding grounds with other marine birds, such as the Peruvian pelican

(*Pelecanus thagus*), Bougainville cormorant (*Phalacrocorax bougainvillii*), and booby (*Sula variegata*), or even settle near colonies of pinnipeds, such as *Otaria byronia* and *Arctocephalus australis*.

Humboldts breed year round, because their breeding season is not contingent upon the seasonal availability of food. However, Humboldts, like Galápagos penguins, do suffer from random variations in water temperature. During El Niño events, the dense fish shoals that Humboldts feed on disappear. These conditions affect the success of their breeding.

The Humboldt's sexual displays have not been studied extensively, but they appear to be similar to those of other *Spheniscus* species. The female lays two pale-green eggs.

Chick-Rearing. Parents take turns guarding and feeding their offspring daily. As soon as the chicks are thermally independent, both parents can forage simultaneously for two days at a time, but one or the other returns daily to feed the young.

Foraging. Upwelling along the Peruvian coast caused by the Humboldt Current increases the density of pelagic fish shoals. Humboldts feed mainly on

Engraulis ringens, Sardinops sagax, Odonthestes regis, and *Scomberesox sp.* In Chile, some penguins also feed on cephalopods (*Todarodes fillipovae*).

Their prey measure between 1.45 and 10.8 inches (3.6 and 27 cm).

During the chick-rearing stage, foraging trips coincide with daylight hours. The parents leave at 6 a.m. and return in the late afternoon. Two o'clock seems to be the busiest time at sea. Humboldts forage in groups of two to five. They alternate between underwater and surface swimming for 20 seconds each. Their average speed is 2.7 miles per hour (4.5 km/h).

An adult and a chick in front of their burrow

The maximum recorded dives are close to 230 feet (70 m), but most birds either remain within 3.3 feet (1 m) of the surface or dive 100 feet (30 m) at a 45° angle, returning immediately to the surface along the same trajectory.

Survival. Volant predators, such as the simeon gull (*Larus belcheri*), the Dominican gull (*Larus dominicanus*), and the skua (*Catharacta chilensis*), prey mostly on eggs and young, unguarded chicks. Mainland Humboldt colonies are also at the mercy of the desert fox (*Dusicyon sechurae*).

Fur seals and sea lions are likely to attack Humboldts, as they do other *Spheniscus* species, although this type of predation has never been confirmed.

Humboldts also have to contend with dramatic drops in their food supply caused by oceanographic oscillations. The Humboldt Current that causes an upwelling of nutrient-rich waters from the bottom of the ocean is sometimes counteracted by a reverse current called El Niño. This unusual event can result in breeding failure, because of the lack of fish needed to feed the young.

Distribution. Humboldts are found along the coastline bathed by the Humboldt Current, from the Chilean Algarrobo Islets (lat. 33° 20' S.), located 27 miles (47 km) south of Valparaiso, down to the Peruvian Foca Island (lat. 5° 12' S.).

They nest on islands and on the mainland. The largest colonies are located on San Juan Point and Pachacamac Island in Peru.

Population. In the 1980s, the Peruvian population was estimated at between 4,500 and 6,000 birds. It is likely to have declined since then due to human interference and El Niño events (see the section on the Galápagos penguin).

Humans are the main culprit in the dramatic decline of the Humboldt's population that has occurred since the middle of the 19th century. The extracting of guano on the Peruvian and Chilean islands destroyed the substratum needed to excavate insulative burrows. The birds have been forced to nest in the open, where they are vulnerable to predators. They have been killed for their skin and meat, and their eggs have been harvested. In an effort to reduce predation by land mammals, the governments have built impassable fences that even foxes can't climb over.

Anchoveta fishing, a leading Peruvian industry in the sixties and seventies, was responsible for the destruction of many Humboldts. Many birds drowned in gill nets, and overfishing led to the reduction of food stocks in the Peruvian waters. In addition, 10,000 or so birds have been exported over the past 32 years to zoos throughout the world.

Humboldts are now considered an endangered species and are protected by the Peruvian government.

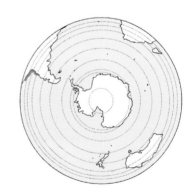

GALÁPAGOS PENGUIN

Spheniscus mendiculus
(Sundevall, 1871)

French: Manchot de Galapagos
German: Galapagospinguin
Norwegian: Galapagospingvin
Flemish: Galapagospinguïn

Description. *Adults:* The Galápagos penguin has a dark-gray back and white underparts. The dorsal pre-molt plumage is brownish due to sun discoloration. Its markings are similar to other penguins of the *Spheniscus* genus but are not as well delineated. A thin, white line runs from above the eyes and curves around the back of the head to join under the chin. An indistinct, black, inverted-horseshoe-shaped band runs from the feet under the flippers and across the upper part of the breast. Males have bolder markings than females. The patch of bare skin at the base of the bill enables individual penguins to recognize each other. The white underparts are sometimes flecked with black feathers. The feet are black. The upper part of the bill is black, and the mandible is white.

Immatures: Fledglings have a gray-and-white plumage with no facial or pectoral markings. They put on their adult plumage six months later, after their first molt.

Chicks: Newly born chicks are covered in gray down with lighter patches around the eyes. The first feathers appear within a week.

Length/Weight: Adults measure around 20 inches (50 cm) in length.

The average weight of the male is 4.6 pounds (2.10 kg). Before molting, he is 5.5 pounds (2.50 kg), and before new feather growth, 3.75 pounds (1.70 kg). The female is slightly smaller and weighs an average of 4.2 pounds (1.90 kg). Before molting, she is 5.3 pounds (2.40 kg), and she is 3.5 pounds (1.60 kg) after incubating.

A Galápagos penguin hunts for prey from the water's surface, Bartholomew Island.

Breeding. The breeding cycle of Galápagos penguins is irregular. The air temperature in this equatorial archipelago remains constant year round and does not regulate the species' breeding rhythm. Oceanographic oscillations, however, have a direct influence on this cycle. The shores of the Galápagos Islands are bathed in differing irregular currents. Only the east/west Cromwell Current along the Peruvian and Ecuadorian coasts creates an environment conducive to breeding, by means of the upwelling of cold, nutrient-rich waters necessary for the development of the food chain. On the other hand, the warmer west/east currents, particularly El Niño, reduce the availability of nutrients closer to the surface by limiting, or even canceling, the continental upwelling. Plankton disperse, leaving birds and marine mammals without sufficient food.

Penguins breed when surface waters are coldest (less than 71.6° F, or 22° C). But breeding can occur year round under favorable conditions. In the Galápagos, 1972 was a tragic year. The strong equatorial countercurrent (El Niño) and the resulting water temperature exceeding 75° F (24° C) caused total breeding failure.

As soon as cold and rich currents return, penguins put on weight and come back to molt on land once they have built up sufficient reserves.

Unlike other *Spheniscidae,* the Galápagos molts before, and sometimes while, nesting. The molt lasts 10 to 15 days. Breeding begins after or during the molt. Molting and breeding are the most energy-consuming periods, requiring a substantial amount of food. If the Cromwell Current is too short, the mortality rate is high. Nonbreeders also molt during the breeding cycle. Molting and breeding generally occur twice a year, although they can sometimes take place every few years.

In such an unpredictable environment, Galápagos penguins breed as often as possible (up to three times a year) to try to maintain a stable population.

The Galápagos Islands are formed by volcanic rock with no deep and malleable substratum. Penguins nest in flat areas where the guano is deep enough to dig a burrow, or in rock crevices and small caves carved out in the lava.

The male brings various nest-building materials to the site (seaweed, leaves, twigs, and so forth), whether they are functional or not.

The newly formed pair engages in a series of mutual displays that are similar to those of other penguin species but not as complex. Mutual preening occurs only when they are breeding. Right before copulation, the male walks around the female, patting her with his flippers; then he forces her down in a prone position, using his body weight. Copulation occurs mainly on land but also in the water.

Incubation begins after the first egg is laid, and lasts 40 days. The second egg is laid three to four days later. Parents take turns incubating. The eggs hatch within two to four days of each other.

Chick-Rearing. Once again, successful

Favorable Conditions

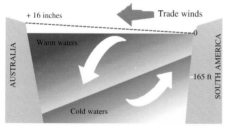

Unfavorable Conditions—El Niño

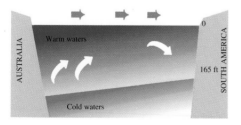

rearing of chicks and chick growth depend on the abundance of nutrients available at the time.

The parents head out to sea in the morning and return in the evening, to take advantage of the cool hours on land. This daily rhythm is similar to that of the Galápagos fur seal (*Arctocephalus galapogoensis*). There is intense competition between the two chicks. The largest one

An adult keeps out of the sun in a rock crevice used as a nest, Cape Douglas, Fernandina Island.

(from the first egg) pecks the back of the head of the weaker sibling until it gives in.

Three weeks after hatching, once the chicks can regulate their body temperature, the parents leave them unguarded.

When they are two months old, the fledglings disperse in the waters around the archipelago.

Foraging. There is little dietary data available for this species. Most of the prey belong to the *Cupleidae* family. These Ecuadorian penguins are avid eaters of sardines, anchovies, and young mullet. Their prey measure 0.4 to 6 inches (1 to 15 cm).

Their foraging habits vary with the hydrographic conditions. The penguins head out to sea between 5 and 7 a.m., returning between 4 and 6:30 p.m. to feed their young and rest. Nonbreeders follow the same schedule, provided there are a sufficient supply of food and favorable weather conditions.

Penguins forage in groups of 50 or so, herding fish shoals with swift acrobatics.

Their dives generally last no more than 30 seconds. The longest dive recorded lasted 79 seconds.

Survival. The Galápagos Islands have varied fauna, and consequently the penguins here have many predators, from the crab to the whale. Sally lightfoot crabs (*Grapsus grapsus*) feed on eggs and chicks. Galápagos snakes (*Dromicus sp.*) attack unguarded eggs and chicks in their nest. Adults are prey to several raptors, such as Galápagos buzzards (*Buteo galapagoensis*), marsh owls (*Asio flammeus*), and white owls (*Tyto alba punctatissima*). There are also many marine preda-

tors: sharks (*Carcharias sp.*), killer whales (*Orcinus orca*), sea lions (*Zalophus californianus wollebacki*), and Galápagos fur seals (*Arctocephalus galapagoensis*). Dogs, cats, and rats, introduced by humans, also prey on these penguins. However, predation is not a major cause of mortality among them, because penguins are none of these species' main prey.

Distribution. Endemic to the Ecuadorian archipelago, the Galápagos penguin nests only on the west coast of Isabela Island (Isabela Bay) and on the shores of Fernandina Island (Espinosa Point).

Population. It is difficult to estimate the population of this cave-nesting species. In 1984, there were 463 and 435 penguins estimated, depending on the season, near breeding grounds. In 1971, there were 1,931 birds. This rapid decline was due to various causes, such as the eruption of Chico volcano on Isabela Island in 1979, dog predation, and an El Niño event in 1982–83.

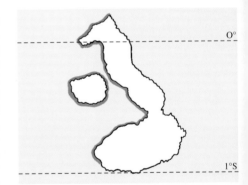

PENGUINS AND PEOPLE: A 6,000-YEAR-OLD HISTORY

THE EXPLOITATION OF PENGUINS

Penguins—anomalous birds, if ever there were any—appeared in seamen's tales at the end of the 15th century. They were not the heroes of these seafaring legends or fables, but simply amusing creatures or an easy source of nourishment. Penguins have never sparked the human imagination, apart from a few obvious anthropomorphic comparisons (the little man in a tuxedo).

Like many other live or extinct species, penguins have suffered atrocities—and still do—at the hands of humans. This began 6,000 years ago, when penguins were found to be an easy and abundant prey.

At the end of the 15th century, explorers sailed the austral seas. Deprived of fresh meat, and stricken by scurvy or on the verge of starvation, they consumed penguin meat, oil, and eggs. The explorers were followed by whalers and sealers, who were ready to do whatever was needed to fill up their tanks with barrels of oil. The blind slaughters were carried out by sailors eager to return to their homeland, but orchestrated by the

Researchers and king penguins cohabit Crozet Island.

shipowners. This exploitation took a great toll on all species.

Penguin populations have also been harmed throughout maritime history by people excavating guano, introducing animals, and so forth.

Let's explore the history of this painful relationship.

Indigenous People and Penguins

Penguins and people have rarely cohabited, but there are five austral regions where they did coexist: in the southern part of South America, on the islands of the South Atlantic, on the coasts of today's South Africa and Namibia, in the south of Australia, and in New Zealand.

In South America, research conducted by Dominique Legoupil of the Musée de l'Homme and Christine Lefebvre of the Museum of Natural History indicates that humans hunted penguins 6,000 years ago in Tierra del Fuego.

The magellanic penguin *(Spheniscus magellanicus),* which still lives in Patagonia, was prey to two indigenous tribes, now extinct. Both lived off the sea and inhabited the shores of the Magellan archipelago, the canals of Chilean Patagonia, Beagle Canal, and the periphery of Tierra del Fuego. They were the Alacalufs (or Qawaskars) and the Yamanas (or Yahgans).

The Alacalufs were poor nomads who traveled by canoe. They caught magellanics nesting in burrows with their bare hands, at the risk of being pinched badly. They dug trenches and built little walls to corner these birds, who were quick on land but unable to fly, and then chased them with clubs. For the Alacalufs, penguin eggs were a prime source of nourishment during nesting season, in November through December. According to some accounts, they hunted penguins not only for food but also for their oil, which they used as combustible, and for their strong pelts, which they turned inside out to make baby carriers and clothes.

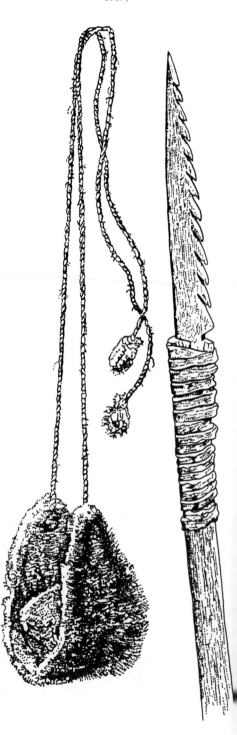

Yamana sling and spear (drawing by Lefebvre, 1989)

Their close neighbors, the Yamanas, used clubs and slings made of seal skin held together with two seal-tendon strings. These hunters were such excellent shots that their prey were unlikely ever to escape. They also hunted from their boats, harpooning penguins that swam nearby. Their spears were made of hardwood *(Nothofagus betuloïdes),* with a sharp, barbed whale bone tied to the tip with seal tendons or skin.

They hunted groups of penguins by barring the entrance of the bay with their canoes and throwing stones in the water to gently herd the birds toward the beach. There, they clubbed the penguins, skinned them, and cut them up; then they roasted them over open flames or baked them in the ashes. They barely cooked the meat. It is difficult to determine the importance of penguins in the Yamanas' diet, but it appears to have been the tribe's fourth most consumed food.

There are still many magellanic penguins around Tierra del Fuego, but both native tribes have disappeared. Archeologists continue to search for traces of these tribes, who vanished into the austral mist without leaving much clue as to how they survived in this inhospitable land on so little.

Three hundred miles to the east of Tierra del Fuego lie the Falkland Islands, an archipelago as large as Belgium. The islands remained uninhabited until the beginning of the 19th century, when they were settled by Europeans who lived off local resources. This land was presumably discovered in the late 16th century by Sir Richard Hawkins, but no one set foot upon it until 1690, according to the log of John Strong, captain of the HMS *Welfare.* In February of 1794, Louis Antoine de Bougainville established a colony on the large, eastern island at Port Louis (lat. 51° 35' S., long. 58° 07' W.). Penguins soon became a valued food source for these people.

Egging is still a popular tradition on some farms from late October to early

Rockhopper egg collecting in the Falklands in the early 20th century, Port Stanley Museum Collection

November. This practice, which has threatened many of the archipelago's penguin colonies (see the section on the rockhopper penguin), is in decline now due to stringent regulations. Among the Falklands' four species, only the gentoo *(Pygoscelis papua)* and the magellanic penguins still suffer from this custom. Egg collectors retrieve magellanic eggs from their burrows by using a special tool made of a stick 6.6 feet (2 m) long with a rigid scoop slightly larger than the egg on the end (about 2.9 inches long by 2.1 inches in diameter, or 7.3 cm long by 5.4 cm). Penguin eggs can be boiled or fried, and are used to make mouthwatering cakes and omelets.

Farther east, in the middle of the Atlantic Ocean, away from any land, lies a small volcanic island called Tristan da Cunha (lat. 37° 05' S., long. 12° 30' W.). The foothills of the volcano are home to a colony of rockhoppers *(Eudyptes chrysocome)* that lived there undisturbed until the beginning of the 19th century. The island, though occasionally visited by seafarers, was uninhabited. In 1814, it was annexed by the British Crown and became a military base. The military later brought in women from St. Helen to keep the men company. These unique people, isolated from the rest of the world, learned not to rely on sporadic supplies from the outside. They used penguins for food and many crafts. The oil extracted from adult penguins was used in lamps, and as a main ingredient in candles and soap. It was also used to protect and waterproof the canvas stretched across the beams of longboats. During molting season, shedded feathers were collected and molting birds were plucked live to provide down for pillows. Women crafted table mats with rockhoppers' yellow plumes and sold them to people aboard visiting ships. They had to strangle 30 penguins or so in order to create one of these embroidery works with ribbons and bows. Bonnets and purses also were crafted in the same style. Islanders ate a great deal of rockhopper eggs and traded them by the barrelful for biscuits and tobacco from visiting ships.

Farther east, in South Africa, archeological research has revealed the importance of penguins in local crafts. In Namibia, near Lüderitz (lat. 26° 35' S., long. 15° 05' E.), researchers uncovered 4,000-year-old megellanic penguin *(Spheniscus demersus)* bones. The gashes found in them indicate that the penguins had been skinned. Seafarer tales confirm this discovery. A 1779 engraving by Colonel Gordon shows Nama tribes, indigenous to the banks of the Orange River (lat. 28° 38' S., long. 16° 24' E.), wearing capes made out of some 50 immature penguin skins. In the early 19th century, Owen, who traveled across Walvis Bay (lat. 23° S., long. 14° 30' E.),

Detail of a 1779 engraving showing a Nama wearing a cape made of penguin skins, Avery, 1985

An 1854 engraving depicting the slaughter of penguins by Maoris, Te Papa Collection, Tongarewa Museum, Wellington

wrote about his encounter with natives clothed in penguin skins. These strong skins were easy to degrease and must have been a choice adornment with their attractive black-and-white markings.

There is very little information regarding the hunting and exploitation of penguins in Australia. There have been some reports in Tasmania of egg collecting in large marine-bird colonies. This collecting coincides with the nesting season of the little penguin *(Eudyptula minor)*. During the summer months, inland and coastal tribes migrated closer to sooty shearwater *(Puffinus griseus)* rookeries that neighbored little penguin breeding grounds.

In New Zealand, archeological studies show the importance of penguins in the Maoris' diet prior to 1500 B.C. Penguin bones often have been excavated on dwelling sites. On North Island, bones from the little penguin were found along with the remains of cormorants, ducks, petrels, and *Rallidae*. On South Island, all current species were found in the excavations of ancient villages, but the

penguins seem to have played a lesser role in the Maoris' diet than on North Island. The Maoris must have eaten *Spheniscidae* only when other fowl was not available, especially on Stewart Island.

However, according to 18th-century naturalists, particularly Joseph Banks, who sailed aboard the *Endeavour* in 1769 with James Cook, penguins were a common food in the Maoris' diet.

Penguins Versus Explorers

For early austral explorers, penguins were a source of many scientific questions and taxonomic descriptions, but also an abundant fount of fresh food and an easy prey. Herded into canoes like sheep or clubbed to death, they saved many a sailor from the dreaded scurvy and famine.

There have been numerous accounts of penguin slaughters throughout history, from Fernando Magellan, William Dampier, James Cook, and many others.

In early 1520, Pigafetta, who chronicled

Fernando Magellan's round-the-world journey, was one of the first to write about penguins, which he called geese: "After following the coast towards the Antarctic pole, they came to two islands full of geese and sea wolves in such numbers that in one hour they were able to fill their five ships with geese, and they are completely black and unable to fly and they live on fish, and are so fat that it is necessary to peel them; they do not have feathers and have a beak like a crow."

William Dampier, a great filibuster and explorer, wrote about penguin meat in his round-the-world travel diary published in 1699: "There are many penguins on this island (Lobos del Mar), such as those I have seen in prodigious numbers throughout the south seas, on the coast of the newly discovered country, and the Cape of Good Hope. Their flesh is mediocre, but their eggs are delicious."

Explorers destroyed islands indiscriminately, trying to kill as many penguins as possible and clear land. The account of Dom Pernetty's journey to the Falklands in 1764 is rather enlightening: "The island that M. de Bougainville set fire to was first

called Penguin Island because of the multitude of penguins there. There were so many that more than two hundred died in the fire. And yet, everywhere we turned, there were countless numbers of them left." The fires burned deep holes in the peaty soil of these austral islands, and the penguins that fell in were unable to climb out.

Cook wrote about penguin hunting during his 1775 journey through the South Seas: "[The penguins we caught] were of the size of small geese, and of that species which is the most common in the neighborhood of the Straits of Magelhaens. The English at the Falkland Islands have named them jumping-jacks. . . . When the whole flock was beset, they all became very bold at once and ran violently at us, biting our legs or any part of our clothes. They are excessively hard-lived, for having left a great number of them seemingly dead on the field of battle, and going in pursuit of the rest, they all at once got up and walked off with great gravity." Cook then described the great penguin slaughters: "There is an amazing number of these amphibious birds (on several islands near the States land), so we could club as many as we chose to. I cannot say whether they are palatable or not. During shortages, we found them delectable, but that was because of the lack of other fresh foods."

Late 19th-century Antarctic explorers continued their predecessors' custom. When their ships were marooned for the winter or as they sailed through, they supplemented their diet of canned foods and dried meat with penguin meat. However, these expeditions were quite different from those of the first explorers and whalers, and it was with reluctance that these men sacrificed the lives of penguins. The health and survival of the crews were at stake.

J.-B. Charcot, aboard the *Pourquoi-Pas?*, confirmed this in his diary notes of February 16, 1909: "Chollet and two crewmen circled the island in a skiff. They came across very few seals, which is rather worrisome. We need oil in order to conserve our coal, which I want to use only sparingly. And I would have liked to store a good amount of meat for the winter. The poor penguins will be the first to suffer, for we will have to sacrifice a hundred or so. I hate these slaughters, but, in our situation, we have no choice. And it is all the more unbearable as these animals are gentle and harmless."

Ruins of the overwintering hut built by the crew of the Antarctic, *Paulet Island, 1903*

Raymond Rallier du Baty, who explored and charted the Kerguelen Islands in 1908, wrote: "We had to kill a few poor birds, because we needed food. Their flesh was not bad, and, in any case, it satisfied our hunger."

The austral islands saw many shipwrecks. The list of shipwrecked seamen who were forced to survive in extreme conditions would fill more than a few pages. John Nunn is a good example.

Nunn spent 27 precarious months with three of his mates lost in the Kerguelen Islands in December of 1825. Clothed in seal skins, and with sea elephant skins for boots, they survived on pinnipeds and birds. They rarely ate penguins, because they found them to be quite disgusting. However, they ate a lot of king and gentoo eggs, and even built a little cart to carry their booty. They spent their time making a variety of objects from bird skins, such as tobacco pouches from the necks of king penguins.

Commander Larsen, captain of the *Antarctic,* which sunk in the Weddell Sea in 1903, spent the winter on Paulet Island with 19 crewmen: "Once we had secured a shelter, we gathered an abundant supply of food at the expense of penguins and seals. The first day's catch was quite good: 326 birds. The next day was even better: 508. We killed a total of 1,100 penguins. So we were not about to starve."

Penguins were most often skinned and cut up on the spot. Only the breasts were saved, and then cooked with the available means. Recipes and names of dishes varied, according to the cooks' talent and the narrators' imagination. Penguins were served cold, fried, stewed, or in pâtés.

Doctor Cook, who, in 1898, overwintered somewhere on the Antarctic ice pack aboard the *Belgica,* described the taste of penguin: "Penguin, as an animal, seems to be mammal, fish, and fowl in equal measure. Its taste can best be described as a combination of beef, a piece of cod, and a duck carcass, stewed in a blood and cod liver oil sauce." The crew of the *Belgica* also used penguin skins to make spats and shoes.

In the spring, the first eggs laid became omelets or were stored in salt. It took little time to collect large numbers of eggs. Borchgrevink wrote in 1901: "In a half-hour, the two Finns collected 435 penguin eggs for our stores."

Shackleton, an Antarctic explorer, recounted the extreme living conditions he and his crew underwent after their ship *Endurance* was crushed in the Weddell Sea in 1917. The men, who were marooned on Elephant Island, discovered another benefit in killing penguins: "When we are lucky enough to find nondigested fish in the penguins' stomach, we cook them in cans suspended over the stove with wires."

Even after these heroic times, penguins were still considered an important food source for personnel at scientific bases isolated during long winter months in the Antarctic and subantarctic islands. Penguins and seals were the only fresh meat available to them.

Raoul Desprez, who cooked for the French polar expedition in Adélie Land from 1950 to 1952, told of different ways penguin was prepared. Emperors (*Aptenodytes forsteri*) were prepared in roasts or steaks. In the case of Adélies, only the "breast supreme" satisfied the members of the expedition. At the beginning of the nesting season, eggs were fixed like chicken eggs—fried, poached, or in omelets.

This custom of people supplementing their diet with penguin meat and eggs lasted for many years, until a number of official organizations called for restrictions in penguin hunting.

The Massive Exploitation of Penguins

In 1848, Dumont d'Urville summed up the seafarer's treatment of penguins: "These poor animals who had nothing to fear, other than the voracity of Antarctic dogs, are now exploited by the Europeans who pull into port in the Falklands."

The industrial exploitation of penguins was not as extensive as that of sea elephants (for oil) or fur seals (for skins), but it was widespread enough at one point in time to greatly impact penguin populations.

The austral sea explorers were followed closely by an armada of ships financed by greedy owners. The hard-core, experienced crews, who were tossed around for months on the heavy seas at high latitudes, had only one goal: to fill their barrels with marine-mammal oil as quickly as possible. Elephant seals (*Mirounga leonina*)—peaceful animals that had no chance of escaping—were slaughtered by the thousands. In order to liquefy such large amounts of fat, the men needed a combustible. Heavy and cumbersome coal was often substituted with a more manageable combustible: penguins. This extremely abundant "firewood" that was available during austral summers helped save on precious coal reserves and, moreover, could be brought to the site without much effort.

In around 1820, English and French whalers stationed in South Georgia for four months fed their furnaces with penguins, throwing them barely unconscious into the fire like logs. At the end of the 19th century, the sealers who exploited the large elephant seal colony on the Kerguelen Islands ran penguins through a press to extract their oil.

As elephant seal populations decreased, penguins were doomed to suffer the rapaciousness of sealers and whalers always searching for extra provisions. The thick blubber that protected the penguins from the cold could easily top up a light load.

All they had to do was slaughter a few thousand birds.

At the end of the 19th century, on Macquarie Island, royal penguins (*Eudyptes schlegeli*) as well as king penguins (*Aptenodytes patagonica*) were herded like sheep into digesters, at a rate of 4,000 birds per day or 150,000 per year. They were clubbed at the foot of the furnace and sometimes thrown in alive. It was not a very lucrative business at a pint of oil per bird and £18 per ton, but the hunt was risk-free.

The slaughter, licensed by the Australian government, came to an end only in 1918, under the pressure of influential explorers, such as Mawson and Hurley, and after the liquidation of the companies responsible for the exploitation.

The consequences of these rapacious killings were catastrophic, with royal penguins becoming nearly extinct.

Oil was extracted from king penguins (*Aptenodytes patagonica*) in South Georgia and used to preserve fur seal (*Arctocephalus gazella*) skins.

In the northwest of the Falklands, on Steeple and Grand Jason Islands, rockhoppers (*Eudyptes chrysocome*) suffered the most. According to I. Strange, nearly 500,000 penguins (*E. chrysocome* and *P. papua*) were killed between 1863 and 1866 to produce 74,360 gallons (286,000 liters) of oil. Around the same period, king penguins disappeared completely from the archipelago.

But the harm caused by the sealers did not stop here.

In the Falkland Islands, seal hunting had many dire consequences for penguins. The dauntless hunters would chase sea lions out from under the tussock grass by setting it afire, burning alive juvenile magellanic penguins that could not escape.

Even in 1955, on Sea Lion Island, carcasses of penguin chicks were found burnt in an ashy lunar landscape.

An easy and abundant prey, penguins suffered many more hardships because of the variety of resources that they provided seasonally.

The species that nested closer to the cities landed in the markets as skins, feathers, meat, or eggs. At the end of the 19th century, Humboldts (*Spheniscus humboldti*) were displayed throughout the markets along the Peruvian coast, and magellanics (*Spheniscus magellanicus*) in the stalls of Buenos Aires and Montevideo.

On Dassen Island, off the coast of South Africa, commercial Cape penguin egging was carried out at a rate of 300,000 eggs per year. Egg collecting was encouraged because it provided an important source of revenue for colonial establishments. From February 15 to August 15, teams of egg collectors armed with wicker baskets moved through the colonies in close order, retrieving from the burrows the precious greenish eggs.

People always seemed to find new ways of exploiting penguins. Another example is the massive use of these birds as bait in lobster traps. This practice was common in South Africa and took a toll on Cape penguins. The same happened on Saint Paul Island (lat. 38° 55' S. , long. 77° 41' E.) during the tests conducted on the exploitation of the island's resources. In 1930, Bretons and Madagascans, hired by the Bossière brothers, shipowners from Le Havre, slaughtered 400 rockhoppers daily to bait the precious lobsters that were destined for the Langouste Française cannery. Not all the slaughtered animals were used; dead bodies littered the area, making it that much more noxious. This useless massacre could have been avoided, because there were plenty of fish near the lobster fishing grounds that could have been used as bait. But penguins were easier to catch. Edgar Aubert de la Rue denounced the company for trying to wipe out the entire colony on the pretext of unfair competition: penguins were feeding on the young lobsters. The death of several lobster fishermen ended the commercial exploitation of this crater lost in the Indian Ocean, putting an end to the fatal project.

At the very beginning of the 19th century, whalers sailing through the Falkland Islands filled their storerooms with thousands of penguin eggs of all species. They dipped the eggs in seal oil and buried them in sand barrels. The barrels were turned over every three days so that the egg shells wouldn't stick together. The oil and sand bound together to form a watertight, sandy crust that helped preserve the valuable food complement for nine months.

Sailors aboard whalers also made slippers out of penguin skins.

Nowadays, penguins are no longer the victims of mass destruction at the hands of sealers and nest robbers, but they have to face far more pernicious human torments: repeated oil spills in South Africa (Cape penguins), mass tourism in Australia (little penguins), encroachment of agricultural land in New Zealand (yellow-eyed penguins), and overfishing in the Falkland Islands.

Schools of krill and squid are an important source of protein in the austral regions, yet they are threatened everywhere. Russian, Spanish, Japanese, and French trawlers dip into this exhaustible supply, which is the only food source for the few surviving whales and the thousands of otaries, seals, and penguins. Many researchers are currently trying to determine the diet of the different penguin species and the biology of their prey. Let us hope that humankind does not repeat its errors. The next time, they could truly be fatal. These animals that took millions of years to adapt to the marine environment could disappear in just a few decades.

A magellanic chick burnt in a tussock grass fire on Sea Lion Island in the Falklands

The Exploitation of Guano

In the 19th century, during the industrial revolution with its many maritime explorations, guano started to appear on the tall sailing ships' bills of lading.

Guano is the name given to the dried droppings deposited by penguins and other fish-eating marine birds, such as cormorants and boobies. Rich in nitrogen and phosphorus, it was considered the ultimate fertilizer in developing countries.

Guano accumulated over many centuries on islands off the coasts of Peru, South Africa, and Tasmania, forming a thick crust that was several feet deep.

Spheniscus penguins—Cape, magellanic, Humboldt, and Galápagos—nest in burrows dug in the guano, protected from the heat of the day. This natural fertilizer was used already by the Incas to boost their crops. Harvested conservatively, the organic substratum renewed itself each year. That is, until 1830 or so, when the Europeans and the Americans discovered that guano could substantially increase the yield of their crops.

Twenty million tons of guano were harvested from Peruvian islands between 1850 and 1875, providing Peru with two billion dollars in revenue.

Thousands of Indians loaded this white gold into the holds of vast fleets of sailing ships. And, of course, the inevitable occurred: the guano didn't renew itself fast enough to make up for the depletion. The amounts of deposits were reduced even further on years when El Niño (the famous warm current that destabilizes resources in the Pacific Ocean) reduced the birds' food supply and produced torrential rains that washed away the excrement. The penguins had no shelter for their offspring and became an easy prey for volant predators. Moreover, their exposed brood could not resist the heat of the summer. Peruvian bird islands have been protected from guano harvesting since the beginning of the century to prevent the total destruction of the sites.

Much of the same occurred in South Africa. The Cape penguin population has decreased dramatically. Few chicks ever fledge because they are constantly harassed by volant predators, such as the Dominican gull (*Larus dominicanus*) and the sacred ibis (*Threskiornis aethiopicus*), and exposed to the blistering sun.

The repopulation of certain colonies has been made possible by placing artificial burrows made of cement and fiber piping on breeding grounds to compensate for the lack of guano.

POLLUTION

Penguins generally live far from any source of pollution, but they spend most of their life in a sea filled with all sorts of industrial waste.

The ever-moving sea and its currents dilute the pollutants, but also redistribute them around the globe. Organic and mineral products from large industries are found thousands of miles from the dissipating areas.

Little is known about the effects of heavy metal and organochlorine compounds, because they are rarely found in high ratios. But we know only too well about the disastrous consequences of oil spills, after having witnessed one too many.

Tests conducted in 1971 show traces of the insecticide DDT (dichloro-diphenyl-trichloroethane) in macaroni penguin livers (maximum 32 ppb) and rockhopper blubber (maximum 260 ppb) in the Kerguelen Islands, located thousands of miles away from the dissipating area. PCB (poly-chloro-byphenyl) also was found in these birds' liver and muscles, and in gentoos. Similar readings showed up in Adélie penguins near MacMurdo Base on Ross Island.

Unlike DDT that is present throughout the austral ocean in similar concentrations, the presence of PCB is directly related to the waste produced by electrical plants and trash incinerators on the bases located near these colonies.

High levels of heavy metals, especially cadmium and mercury, were found in Gough Island (South Atlantic) rockhoppers' liver and blubber. Such high concentrations can either result from natural causes, such as the proximity of intense volcanic activity (cadmium is present in the earth crust), or from man-made causes, such as the accumulation of pollutants in a long food chain. Cadmium is used in plastics and battery parts. It concentrates in birds' kidneys and is responsible for lesions in marine birds.

Crude oil is a different story. Most penguin species live far from tankers' shipping lanes, except for Cape penguins, who, in 1987, watched 760,000 tons of petroleum sail past their colonies, coming from the Arab-Persian Gulf and bound for the United States.

This species was the victim of many oil slicks. Several maritime accidents occurred in 1967 near the Cape of Good Hope, because of increased traffic off the tip of South Africa during the Israeli-Arab war, when the Suez Canal was closed.

Risks of oil spillage are not as high elsewhere, but almost everyone remembers the sinking of the *Bahia Paraiso* off the Antarctic Peninsula. The oil that spilled from the ship's tanks polluted the shores where colonies of Adélie penguin were breeding. That year, there was an abundance of krill in the area, and the penguins had to settle for a diet of polluted crustaceans.

Oil drilling on the coast of Argentina caused a great deal of pollution. The waste, leaks, and spills from onshore plants killed many thousands of magellanic penguins.

Oil spills are so dramatic that we tend to forget about regular ballast discharges from tankers and trawlers, and the leaks at bases and in old whaling stations that caused chronic pollution in South Georgia and in the Falklands, after the Falkland war.

In December of 1991, on the Argentinean shores of Patagonia, 16,000 penguins were found oiled, although no spill was ever reported.

The toxicity of petroleum is not always the greatest problem for these birds, except in the case of oil and light hydrocarbons spills. It is the intensive preening that causes the oiled birds to ingest a large amount of pollutants, creating lesions in their stomach and kidneys. These toxic products, when ingested before egg laying, may cause breeding failure. The oil also reduces the insulative properties of penguins' feathers. Their heartbeat and metabolism increases dramatically, because they must exert more energy in order to maintain their body temperature, especially in the water. This abnormal increase in their metabolism depletes their fat reserves. When they are no longer able to maintain their body temperature because all the fat has been burnt off, they eventually die of hypothermia.

Oil Spills That Affected Penguin Populations

Year	Origin	Site	Species
1968	Esso Essen tanker	South Africa	Cape penguin
1968	World Glory tanker	South Africa	Cape penguin
1970	Kazimah tanker	South Africa	Cape penguin
1971	Wafra tanker	South Africa	Cape penguin
1972	Oswego Guardian tanker	South Africa	Cape penguin
1974	Oriental Pioneer tanker	South Africa	Cape penguin
1976	Onshore drilling	Argentina	Magellanic penguin
1978	Pantelis de Lemos tanker	Argentina	Magellanic penguin
1983	Castillo de Belver tanker	South Africa	Cape penguin
1988	Nellan Dan research vessel	Macquarie Is.	Gentoo penguin
			King penguin
			Royal penguin
			Macaroni penguin
1989	Bahia Paraiso supply vessel	Antarctic Peninsula	Adélie penguin
1989	Humboldt research vessel	South Shetlands	
1994	Apollo Sea ore ship	South Africa	Cape penguin

An emperor adult and chick in Adélie Land

APPENDIX

Distribution of Penguins in
Austral Islands and Archipelagos

	Location	Latitude	Longitude
1	Falkland Islands	51°45'	59°00'W
2	South Georgia	54°15'	36°45'W
3	Bouvet Island	54°26'	03°25'E
4	Marion Island	46°36'	37°55'E
5	Crozet Islands	46°30'	51°00'E
6	Kerguelen Islands	49°15'	69°10'E
7	Heard Island	53°00'	73°35'E
8	Amsterdam Island	37°57'	77°40'E
9	St. Paul Island	38°55'	77°41'E
10	Tristan da Cunha Islands	37°05'	12°17'W
11	Gough Island	40°20'	10°00'W
12	South Sandwich Islands	56°00'	26°30'W
13	South Orkney Islands	60°35'	45°30'W
14	South Shetland Islands	62°00'	59°00'W
15	Macquarie Island	54°30'	158°30'E
16	Campbell Island	52°20'	169°10'E
17	Auckland Island	50°35'	166°10'E
18	Snares Islands	48°00'	166°35'E
19	Stewart Island	47°00'	167°50'E
20	Antipodes Islands	49°40'	178°50'E
21	Balleny Islands	66°35'	162°50'E
22	Ross Island	77°30'	168°00'E
23	Roosevelt Island	79°30'	162°00'E
24	Phillip Island	37°49'	147°58'E
25	Tasmania	43°00'	147°00'E
26	Chatham Islands	44°00'	176°30'E
27	Bounty Islands	47°45'	179°05'E
28	Galápagos Islands	00°30'	90°30'E
29	Juan Fernandez Islands	33°00'	80°00'W
30	Diego Ramirez Island	56°30'	68°44'W
31	States Islands	54°47'	64°15'W

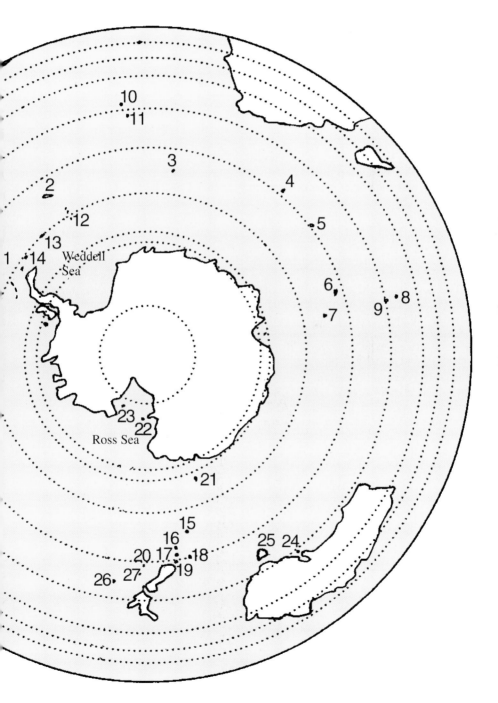

Weddell Sea

Ross Sea

Introduction to Austral Oceanography

The austral ocean forms a ring of water around Antarctica. Its southern limit is the continent itself, and its northern limit, a physicochemical barrier called the Antarctic Convergence (approximately lat. 40° S.). This ocean is connected to the world's three major oceans, which feed it with warmer waters deep below the surface.

The average depth of this immense ocean is 13,200 feet (4,000 m).

The ocean floor's topography shows three basins separated by 6,600-foot (2,000-m) barriers: the Atlantico-Indian basin stretches between the Scotia Arc and the Kerguelen plateau, the Antarctico-Indian basin is located between the Kerguelen plateau and the Balleny rim, and the Pacific-Antarctic basin comprises the rest of the ocean floor.

The austral ocean is 40 million years old. It was formed by the receding of continental masses (Gondwana), which created a circular, eastward-flowing current: the Antarctic Circumpolar Current. The main hydrological characteristic of the austral ocean, this current is activated by westerly winds. Its average flow is estimated to be four times the Gulf Stream's and 400 times the Mississippi's.

This cold and less saline current, deflected northward under the impulse of the Coriolis force, meets the warmer and saltier subantarctic waters around latitude 60° S. This barrier, called the Antarctic Polar Front, plays a significant role in defining the ocean's unique characteristics. Marked by a considerable drop in surface-water temperature, it is where waters from the two masses merge deep below the surface. The cold waters flow under the warmer waters, forming the intermediate Antarctic waters, which then flow northward beyond the Antarctic Convergence.

Different animal species that adapted to specific resources and temperatures have evolved in these two zones. The Antarctic Circumpolar Current branches out under the influence of the barriers separating the ocean-floor basins and the sway of the Coriolis force (induced by the Earth's rotation) that deflects northward the waters flowing westward.

These northward-flowing currents bathe the shores of nearby continents. The most important are the (1) Humboldt Current (Chilean coast), (2) Falkland Current, (3) Benguela Current (west coast of South Africa), (4) West Australian Current, (5) Tasmanian Current, and (6) Southland Current. The combination of these surface currents, the varying densities of water masses, and the prevailing easterly winds create a depression that allows the cold and deep, nutrient-rich waters to rise to the surface. This upwelling produces rich ecosystems south of South Africa, south of Australia and New Zealand, and near the coasts of South America.

An opposing westward current flows near the Antarctic continent under the influence of prevailing winds. The Coriolis effect is reversed, causing the two opposing hydrological flows to meet and push each other back in a zone called the Antarctic Divergence. This repulsion produces a depression that allows the upwelling of deep waters from neighboring oceans. These deep waters are warm and salty, and rich in essential nutrients, such as phosphates, nitrates, and silicates, gleaned from the ocean floor. The warmer surface water creates nutrient-rich polynyas (areas of open water surrounded by sea ice), such as the one in the Weddell Sea.

Near the ice pack, a cold and dense water mass, charged with the salt expelled during the formation of the ice pack, drops to the bottom of the ocean. It cools and oxygenates the deep waters, pushing the warmer waters to the surface.

It is also partially responsible for cooling the oceans of the world 35.6° F (2° C), as it travels northward to the equator.

Sixty-six percent of the austral ocean ices over during the austral winter. The layer of ice blocks ultraviolet sunrays, limiting the thermal and gaseous ex-changes between the water and the air. Algae proliferates in the low light under the 6.6 feet (2 m) of ice.

This unique hydrological pattern determines the distribution of the different penguin species.

Simplified Map of Surface Currents in the Austral Ocean

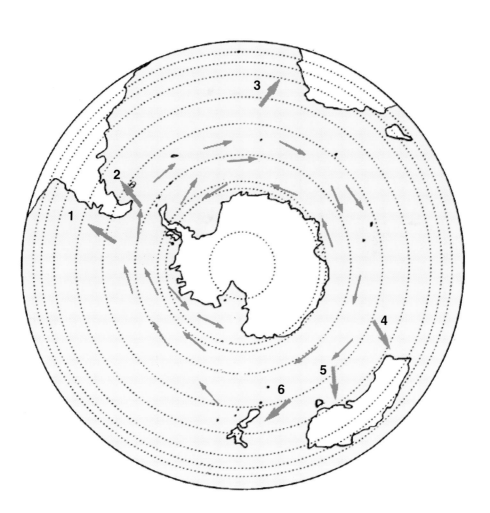

Tussock Grass

Tussock grass thrives in South Georgia, Tierra del Fuego, States Island, Gough Island, and the Falkland Islands. It grows in clumps 12 to 24 inches (30 to 60 cm) apart, and it has a broad root structure, from which grow long, thin blades that are 3.3 to 6.6 feet (1 to 2 m) long. Tussock is extremely resistant to the violent winds that rage under these latitudes.

The root structure grows larger as the plant grows older. The bright-green, clumped leaves dry out over time, although they often stay attached to the roots for several years.

Tussock offers a good example of plant adaptation to a subantarctic environment, and the efficiency of photosynthesis at temperatures near or below 32° F (0° C). The green leaves persist during the winter, enabling the plant to get an early start in the spring before the snow melts. Tussock flowers in October. Pollen is released two months later, and the seeds are scattered in February through March, at the end of the austral summer. The plant reaches its maximum height in January through February, when the temperature is warmest (up to 71.6° F [22° C] on sunny days). Tussock grows only along the coast, because it has a high tolerance for salt water (although it doesn't need much sodium to grow) and it thrives on the nutrients from the sea. Thus, it avoids competing with other plants that could eventually take over.

In the Falkland Islands, it would be impossible to describe tussock grass without bringing up the many animals that breed, feed, and sleep in it. Everywhere can be heard the rustling of wings, shrill whistles, padding on the dried grasses, and raucous cries. Every level of the plant is inhabited, from 4.3 to 6.6 feet (1.3 to 2 m) below the ground to 8.25 to 9.9 feet (2.5 to 3 m) above it. Little petrels (*Pelecanoides urinatrix, Procellaria aequinoctialis, Puffinus gravis*) share the

underground with magellanic penguins (*Spheniscus magellanicus*).

At ground level, geese (*Chloephaga hybrida*), steamer ducks (*Tachyeres brachydactyla*), Turkish vultures (*Cathartes aura*), and *Eudyptes* penguins (*Eudyptes chrysocome, Eudyptes schlegeli*) hide from the elements at the base of the plant.

Little wrens (*Cistothorus platensis*), nightingales, and tussock birds (*Cinclodes antarcticus*) nest in cracks in the base of the plant.

Larger birds, such as the night heron (*Nycticorax nycticorax*), the marsh owl (*Asio flammeus*), and the striated caracara (*Phalcoboenus australis*), nest on top of the thallus and at the base of the leaves.

Pinnipeds also seek shelter under this dense vegetation. Sea elephants (*Mirounga leonina*) sometimes move far inland to molt among the tussock, as do sea lions (*Otaria byronia*) and fur seals.

Birds and marine mammals help the grass thrive by bringing with them a great deal of nutrients. After the big mammals leave, a green algae (*Prasiola crispa*) appears at the base of the plant, within which seeds can

A vertical section of a magellanic's nest dug under a clump of tussock grass

germinate. In return, the base of the leaves that is rich in carbohydrate provides food for some of the animals.

However, animals can also harm this biotope. In South Georgia, the proliferation of fur seals (*Arctocephalus gazella*) resulted in soil erosion and halted plant growth. Groups of sea lions (*Mirounga leonina*) can also destroy the grass at the height of its growing season.

But domesticated animals, such as cows and sheep, are certainly the greatest threat of all. Imported to the islands in great numbers, they graze much of the grass, especially during lean months.

People also have contributed to the destruction of the grass by setting fire to it in order to clear the land for crops or to chase seals.

Tussock is preserved in certain areas to provide shelter for many magellanic penguins, Falkland Islands.

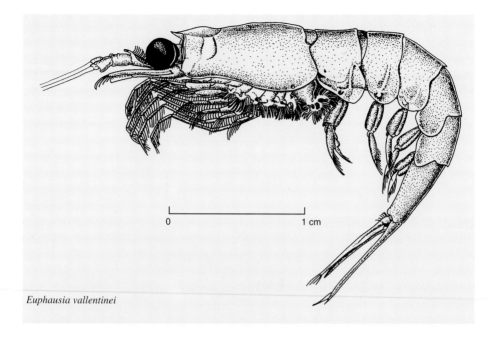

Euphausia vallentinei

Krill

Krill is the generic name given to arthropodous crustaceans from the *Euphausiacea* family, and more specifically to identify *Euphausia superba,* Antarctic krill. The word "krill" comes from old Norwegian and refers to tiny, swarming animals (vermin).

Other species occur in subantarctic waters, such as *E. vallentinei* and *E. lucens,* among 10 others. These little crustaceans measure 1.2 to 2.4 inches (3 to 6 cm) in length and look like shrimp. They are generally red-orange, because of the carotene in their pigment-bearing cells. Swarms of krill can color the sea a brownish rose. At night, luminescent cells transform the swarms into a silvery, iridescent mass.

E. superba is the most abundant animal species on Earth. Its population is estimated at 600,000 billion individuals, which can be translated into 650 million tons.

Krill feed on phytoplankton (diatom, dinoflagellate, microphytoplankton). Its distribution and cycle are closely tied to the proliferation of these plant organisms. *E. superba* occurs in regions covered by a winter ice pack and swept by easterly winds. It is present there year round and relocates within that sphere as needed in order to take advantage of all resources. Krill feed in swarms by swimming against the current at 0.33 to 0.50 feet per second. They can cover many square miles, filtering the suspended particles as they go.

In winter, these grazers take refuge under the sea ice, where they feed on the algae. Twice a year, the females lay two to 300,000 eggs, which sink 2,475 feet (750 m) to the bottom of the sea. The eggs hatch in the abyss. The larvae take two to three years to reach the surface and their adult size of approximately 2.4 inches (6 cm).

Euphausia superba is an essential element in the Antarctic food chain. It predominates the diet of baleen whales (one ton every day for rorquals, *Balenoptera physalus*), crab-eating seals (*Lobodon carcinophagus*), fur seals (*Arctocephalus gazella*), and most penguins and marine birds.

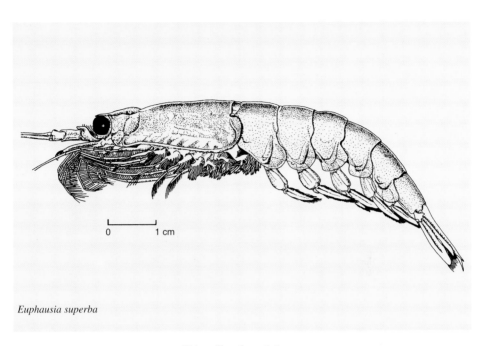

Euphausia superba

Distribution Maps

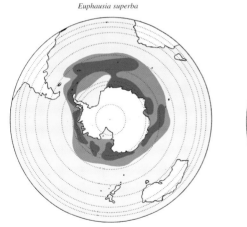

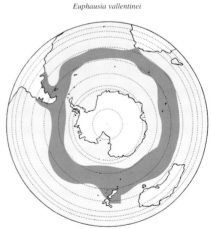

People started fishing for krill in 1972, because it is a good source of protein and vitamins. Trawling grounds are located in South Georgia, the South Orkneys, and the northern coast of the South Shetlands. In 1981–82, the catches were the highest they had ever been: 500,000 tons.

Nowadays, catches total about 350,000 or 400,000 tons per year, 80 percent by the countries of the former Soviet Union. Though krill is mostly used in flour form for feeding livestock, Norwegians, Russians, Chileans, and Japanese also eat krill in fish sticks or in soups.

Plates of Selected Prey Species
(Adult Size)

Pagothenia borchgrevinki

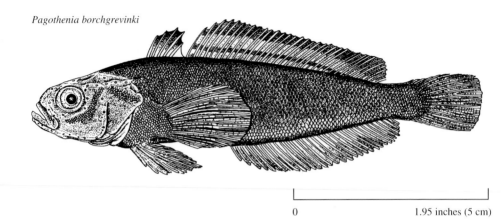

0   1.95 inches (5 cm)

Pleuragramma sp.

0   1.95 inches (5 cm)

Notothenia (Lepidonototheni) squamifrons

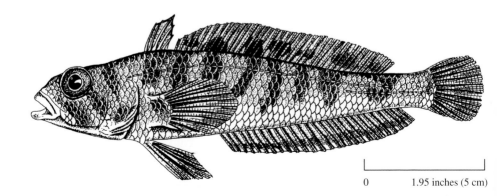

0   1.95 inches (5 cm)

136

Paranotothenia magellanica

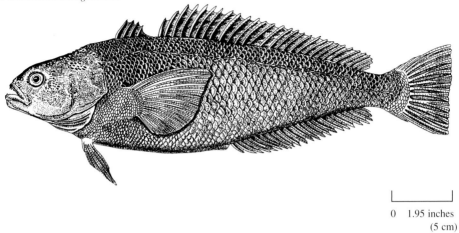

0   1.95 inches
     (5 cm)

Notothenia rossii

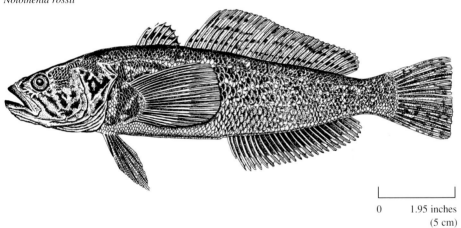

0   1.95 inches
     (5 cm)

Atherina sp.

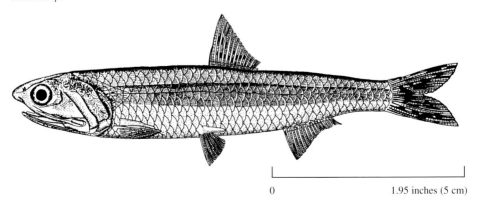

0   1.95 inches (5 cm)

Sardinops sagax

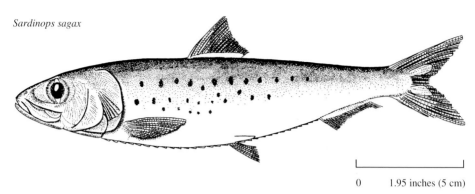

0   1.95 inches (5 cm)

Notolepis coatsi

0 1.95 inches
(5 cm)

Kreffichthys andersoni

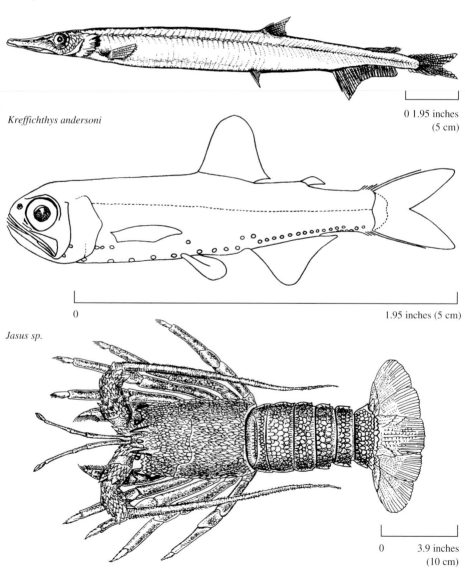

0   1.95 inches (5 cm)

Jasus sp.

0   3.9 inches
(10 cm)

Thermisto gaudichaudii

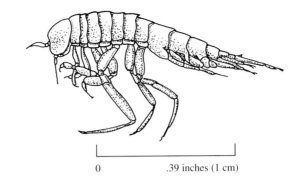

0   .39 inches (1 cm)

Loligo opalesceus

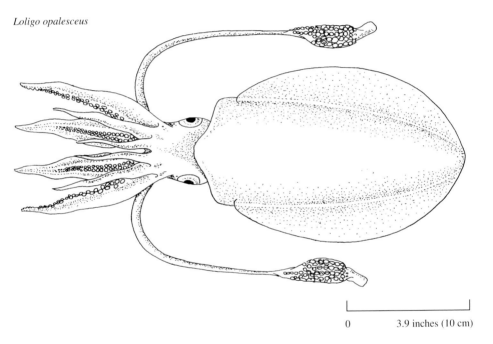

0   3.9 inches (10 cm)

F/Cranchidae
Galiteuthis glacialis

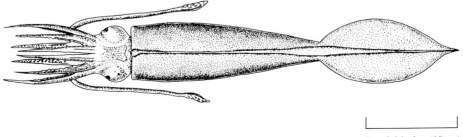

0   3.9 inches (10 cm)

139

Psychroteuthis glacialis

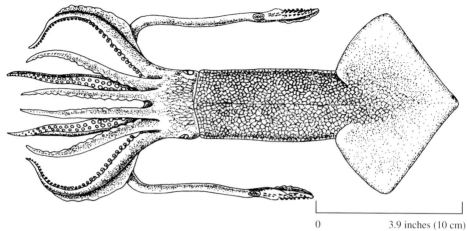

0   3.9 inches (10 cm)

Todarodes filipovae

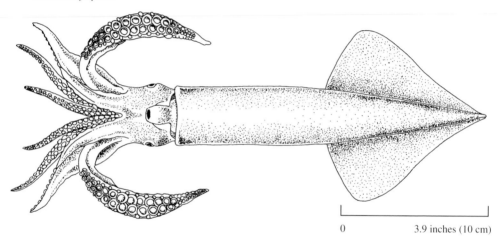

0   3.9 inches (10 cm)

Moroteuthis ingens

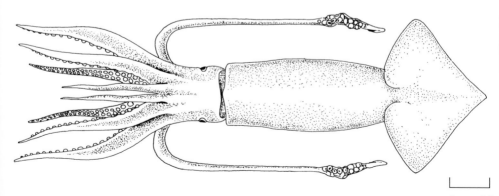

0   3.9
       inches
       (10 cm)

Comparative
Head Drawings

Emperor penguin

King penguin

Adélie penguin

Gentoo penguin

Chinstrap penguin

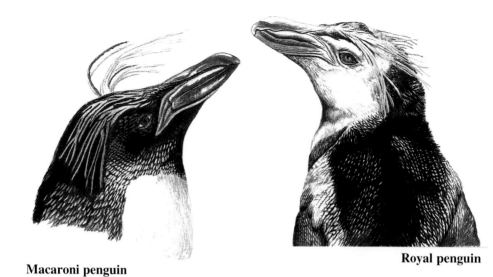

Macaroni penguin

Royal penguin

Fiordland penguin

Snares penguin

Erect-crested penguin

Rockhopper penguin

142

Little penguin

Yellow-eyed penguin

Magellanic penguin

Galápagos penguin

Humboldt penguin

African penguin

143

Bibliography

Emperor Penguin: *Aptenodytes forsteri*

Kooyman, G.L., and Ponganis, P.J. 1990. Behavior and physiology of diving in emperor and king penguins. In *Penguin Biology*, ed. by L.S. Davis and J.T. Darby, Academic Press, 229–242.

Offredo, C., Ridoux, V., and Clarke, M.R. 1985. Cephalopods in the diet of emperor and Adélie penguins in Adélie Land, Antarctica. *Marine Biology* 86: 199–202.

Robertson, G. 1992. Population size and breeding success of the emperor penguin, *Aptenodytes forsteri*, at Auster and Taylor glacier colonies, Mawson Coast, Antarctica. *Emu* 92 (2): 65–71.

Stonehouse, B. 1953. The emperor penguin, *Aptenodytes forsteri*, Gray I-Breeding behavior and development. *F.I.D.S. Sci. Rep.* 6: 33.

King Penguin: *Aptenodytes patagonica*

Adams, N.J. 1984. Utilization efficiency of a squid diet by adult king penguins, *Ptenodytes patagonicus*. *The Auk* 101, n. 4: 884–886.

Adams, N.J. 1987. Foraging range of king penguins, *Aptenodytes patagonicu*, during summer at Marion Island. *J. Zool.* (London) 212: 475–482.

Cherel, Y., and Ridoux, V. 1992. Prey species and nutritive value of food fed during summer to king penguin, *Aptenodytes patagonica*, chicks at Possession Island, Crozet Archipelago. *Ibis* 134: 118–127.

Cherel, Y., Stahl, J-C., and Le Maho, Y. 1987. Ecology and physiology of fasting in king penguin chicks. *The Auk* 104: 254–262.

Groscolas, R. 1990. Metabolic adaptations to fasting in emperor and king penguins. In *Penguin Biology*, ed. by L.S. Davis and J.T. Darby. Academic Press, 269–292.

Hindell, M.A. 1988. The diet of the king penguin, *Aptenodytes patagonicus*, at Macquarie Island, *Ibis* 130: 193–203.

Hunter, S. 1991. The impact of avian predator-scavengers on the king penguin at Marion Island, *Ibis* 133: 343–350.

Kooyman, G.L., and Ponganis, P.J. 1990. Behavior and physiology of diving in emperor and king penguins. In *Penguin Biology*, ed. by L.S. Davis and J.T. Darby, Academic Press, 229–242.

Stonehouse, B. 1960. The king penguin, *Aptenodytes patagnoica*, of South Georgia. I-Breeding behavior and development. *F.I.D.S. Sci. Rep.* 23: 81.

Weimerskirch, H., Stahl, J.C., and Jouventin, P. 1992. The breeding biology and population dynamics of king penguins, *Aptenodytes patagonica*, on the Crozet Islands. *Ibis* 134: 107–117.

Fiordland Penguin: *Eudyptes pachyrhynchus*

Brothers, N.P., and Skira, I.J. 1984. The weka on Macquarie Island. *Notornis* 31: 145–154.

St. Clair, C.C., and St. Clair, R.C. 1992. Weka predation on eggs and chicks of Fiordland crested penguins. *Notornis* 39: 60–63.

Van Heezik, Y.M. 1989. Diet of the Fiordland crested penguin during the post-guard phase of chick growth. *Notornis* 36: 151–156.

Van Heezik, Y.M. 1990. Diet of yellow-eyed, Fiordland crested, and little blue penguin, breeding sympatrically on Codfish Island, New Zealand. *N.Z.J. Zool.* 17: 543–548.

Macaroni Penguin: *Eudyptes chrysolophus*

Brown, C.R. 1986. Feather growth, mass loss, and duration of molt in macaroni and southern rockhopper penguins. *Ostrich* 57: 180–184.

Brown, C.R. 1988. Egg temperature and embryonic metabolism of A- and B-eggs of macaroni and southern rockhopper penguins. *S. Afr. Tydskr. Dierk* 23 (3): 166–172.

Brown, C.R. 1989. Energy requirements and food consumption of *Eudyptes* penguins at the Prince Edward Islands. *Antarctic Science* 1 (1): 15–21.

BROWN, C.R., and KLAGES, N.T. 1987. Seasonal and annual variation in diets of macaroni, *Eudyptes chrysolophus*, penguins at subantarctic Marion Island. *J. Zool.* (London) 212: 7–28.

Croxall, J.P., Briggs, D.R., Karo, A., Nuito, Y., Watanuki, Y., and Williams, T.D. 1993. Diving pattern and performance in the macaroni penguin, *Eudyptes chrysolophus*. *J. Zool.* 230: 31–47.

Williams, T.D. 1989. Aggression, incubation behavior, and egg loss in macaroni penguins, *Eudyptes chrysolophus*, at South Georgia. *Oikos* 55: 19–22.

Williams, T.D. 1990. Growth and survival in macaroni penguins, *Eudyptes chrysolophus*, A- and B-chicks: do females maximize investment in the large B-egg? *Oikos* 58: 349–354.

Williams, T.D., and Croxall, J.P. 1991. Annual variation in breeding biology of macaroni penguins, *Eudyptes chrysolophus*, at Bird Island, South Georgia. *J. Zool.* (London) 223: 189–202.

Royal Penguin: *Eudyptes schlegeli*

Horne, R.S.C. 1985. Diet of royal and rockhopper penguins at Macquarie Island. *Emu:* 150–156.

Shaughnessy, P.D. 1975. Variations in facial colors of the royal penguin. *Emu:* 147–152.

Bibliography

Rockhopper Penguin: *Eudyptes chrysocome*

Bingham, M. 1994. Numbers drop dramatically as our rockhoppers starve. *Penguin News.*

Brown, C.R. 1984. Resting metabolic rate and energetic cost of incubation in macaroni penguins (*Eudyptes chrysolophus*) and rockhopper penguins (*E. chrysocome*). *Comp. Biochem. Physiol.* 77A: 335–350.

Brown, C.R. 1985. Energetic cost of molt in macaroni penguins (*Eudyptes chrysolophus*) and rockhopper penguins (*E. chrysocome*). *J. Comp. Physiol.* B, 155: 515–520.

Brown, C.R. 1986. Feather growth, mass loss, and duration of molt in macaroni and southern rockhopper penguins. *Ostrich* 57: 180–184.

Brown, C.R. 1987. Traveling speed and foraging range of macaroni and rockhopper penguins. *J. Field Ornithol.* 58 (2): 118–125.

Brown, C.R. 1987. Energy requirements for growth and maintenance in macaroni and rockhopper penguins. *Polar Biol.* 8: 95–102.

Brown, C.R. 1988. Egg temperature and embryonic metabolism of A- and B-eggs of macaroni and southern rockhopper penguins. *S. Afr. Tydskr. Dierk.* 23 (3): 166–172.

Brown, C.R. 1989. Energy requirements and food consumption of *Eudyptes* penguins at the Prince Edward Islands. *Antarctic Science* 1 (1): 15–21.

Brown, C.R., And Klages, N.T. 1987. Seasonal and annual variation in diets of macaroni (*Eudyptes chrysolophus chrysolophus*) and southern rockhopper (*E. chrysocome chrysocome*) penguins at subantarctic Marion Island. *J. Zool.* (London) 212: 7–28.

Croxall, J.P., Prince, P.A., Baird, A., and Ward, P. 1985. The diet of the southern rockhopper penguin, *Eudyptes chrysocome chrysocome*, at Beauchêne Island, Falkland Islands. *J. Zool., London* (A), 206: 485–496.

Richardson, M.E. 1984. Aspects of the ornithology of the Tristan da Cunha group and Gough Island, 1972–1974. *Cormorant* 12: 125–197.

Erect-Crested Penguin: *Eudyptes sclateri*

Warham, J. 1972. Aspects of the biology of the erect-crested penguin, *Eudyptes sclateri*. Ardea: 145–184.

Yellow-Eyed Penguin: *Megadyptes antipodes*

Darby, J.T., And Seddon, P.J. 1990. Breeding biology of yellow-eyed penguins, *Megadyptes antipodes*. In *Penguin Biology*, ed. by L.S. Davis and J.T. Darby, Academic Press, 45–61.

Moore, P.J. 1992. Breeding biology of the yellow-eyed penguin, *Megadyptes antipodes,* on Campbell Island. *Emu* 92: 157–162.

Moore, P.J., And Moffat, R.D. 1992. Predation of the yellow-eyed penguin by hooker's sea lion. *Notornis* 39: 68–69.

Seddon, P.J. 1989. Patterns of nest relief during incubation and incubation period variability in the yellow-eyed penguin, *Megadyptes antipodes*. *N.Z.J. Zool.* 16: 393–400.

Seddon, P.J. 1990. Activity budget for breeding yellow-eyed penguins. *N.Z.J. Zool.* 17: 527–532.

Seddon, P.J. 1990. Behavior of yellow-eyed penguin chicks. *J. Zool.* (London) 220: 333–343.

Seddon, P.J., and Davis, L.S. 1989. Nest-site selection by the yellow-eyed penguin. *The Condor* 91: 653–659.

Seddon, P.J., and Van Heezik, Y. 1990. Diving depths of the yellow-eyed penguin, *Megadyptes antipodes, Emu* 90: 53–57.

Van Heezik, Y. 1990. Patterns and variability of growth in the yellow-eyed penguin. *The Condor* 92: 904–912.

Van Heezik, Y. 1990. Seasonal, geographical, and aged-related variations in the diet of the yellow-eyed penguin, *Megadyptes antipodes*. *N.Z.J. Zool.* 17: 201–212.

Van Heezik, Y. 1990. Diet of yellow-eyed, Fiordland crested, and little blue penguins, breeding sympatrically on Codfish Island, New Zealand. *N.Z.J. Zool.* 17: 543–548.

Van Heezik, Y., and Davis, L. 1989. Effects of food variability on growth rates, fledging sizes, and reproductive success in the yellow-eyed penguin, *Megadyptes antipodes*. *Ibis* 132: 354–365.

Van Heezik, Y., and Seddon, P. 1989. Stomach sampling in the yellow-eyed penguin: erosion of otoliths and squid beaks. *J. Field Ornithol.* 60 (4): 451–458.

Adélie Penguin: *Pygoscelis adeliae*

Ainley, D.G., Leresche, R.E., and Sladen ,W.J.L. 1983. *Breeding Biology of the Adélie Penguin.* University of California Press.

Chapell, M.A., and Souza, S.L. 1988. Thermoregulation, gas exchange, and ventilation in the Adélie penguin, *Pygoscelis adeliae*. *J. Comp. Physiol.* B, 157: 783–790.

Culik, B., and Wilson, R.P. 1991. Energetics of underwater swimming in Adélie penguins, *Pygoscelis adeliae*. *J. Comp. Physiol.* B, 161: 285–291.

Culik, B., and Wilson, R.P. 1991. Swimming energetics and performance of instrumented Adélie penguins, *Pygoscelis adeliae*. *J. Exp. Biol.* 158: 355–368.

Culik, B., Wilson, R.P., Dannfeld, R., Adelung, D., Spairani, H.J., and Coria, N.R. 1991. *Pygoscelid* penguins in a swim canal. *Polar Biol.* 11: 277–282.

Culik, B., Woakes, A.J., Adelung, D., Wilson, R.P., Coria, N.R., and Spairani, H.J. 1990. Energy requirements of Adélie penguin, *Pygoscelis adeliae*. *J. Comp. Physiol.* B, 160: 61–70

Culik, B.M. 1987. Fluoride turnover in Adélie penguins, *Pygoscelis adeliae*, and other bird species. *Polar Biol.* 7: 179–187.

Culik, B.M., Heise, D., Adelung, D., Wilson, R.P., Coria, N.R., and Spairani, H.J. 1989. In situ heart rate and activity of incubating Adélie penguins, *Pygoscelis adeliae*. *Polar Biol.* 9: 365–370.

Davis, L.S., and Miller, G.D. 1990. Foraging patterns of Adélie penguins during the incubation period. In *Antarctic Ecosystems, Ecological Change and Conservation*, ed. by K.R. Kerry and G. Hempel, Springer Verlag.

Lishman, G.S. 1985. The comparative breeding biology of Adélie and chinstrap penguins, *Pygoscelis adeliae* and *P. antarctica*. *Ibis* 127: 84–99.

Muller-Schwarze, D., and Muller-Schwarze, C. 1975. Relations between leopard seals and Adélie penguins. *Rapp. P.V. Reun.* CIEM 169: 394–404.

Murray, Levick G. 1914. *Antarctic Penguins*, ed. by W. Heineman.

Ridoux, V., and Offredo, C. 1989. The diets of five summer breeding seabirds in Adélie Land, Antarctica, *Polar Biol.* 9: 137–145.

Sadleir, R.M.F., and Lay, K.M. 1991. Foraging movements of Adélie penguins, *Pygoscelis adeliae*, in McMurdo Sound. In *Penguin Biology*, ed. by Lloyd S. Davis and John T. Darby, Academic Press, 157–179.

Trivelpiece, W.Z., and Trivelpiece, S.G. 1991. Courtship period of Adélie, gentoo, and chinstrap penguins. In *Penguin Biology*, ed. by Lloyd S. Davis and John T. Darby, Academic Press, 113–127.

Wilson, R.P., and Culik, B.M. 1991. The cost of a hot meal: facultative specific dynamic action may ensure temperature homeostasis in post-ingestive endotherms. *Comp. Biochem. Physiol.* 100A, n. 1: 151–154.

Wilson, K.J., Taylor, R.H., and Barton, K.J. 1990. The impact of man on Adélie penguins at Cape Halett, Antarctica. In *Antarctic Ecosystems, Ecological Change and Conservation*, ed. by K.R. Kerry and G. Hempel, Springer Verlag.

Wilson, R.P., and Wilson, M-P.T.J. 1989. Tape: a package-attachment technique for penguins. *Wildl. Soc. Bull.* 17: 77–79.

Wilson, R.P., Culik, B.M., Coria, N.R., Adelung, D., and Spairani, H.J. 1989. Foraging rhythms in Adélie penguins, *Pygoscelis adeliae*, at Hope Bay, Antarctica; determination and control. *Polar Biol.* 10: 161–165.

Wilson, R.P., Culik, B.M., Adelung, D., Spairani, H.J., and Coria, N.R. 1991. Depth utilization by breeding Adélie penguins, *Pygoscelis adeliae*, at Esperanza Bay, Antarctica. *Marine Biology* 109: 181–189.

Wilson, R.P., Culik, B.M., Adelung, D., Corian, N.R., and Spairani, H.J. 1990. Packages for attachment to seabirds: what color do Adélie penguins dislike least? *J. Wildl. Manage.* 54 (3): 447–451.

Wilson, R.P., Culik, B.M., Adelung, D., Corian, N.R., and Spairani, H.J. 1991. To slide or strike: when should Adélie penguins, *Pygoscelis adeliae*, toboggan? *Can. J. Zool.* 69: 221–225.

Gentoo Penguin: *Pygoscelis papua*

Adams, N.J., and Brown, C.R. 1983. Diving depth of the gentoo penguin, *Pygoscelis papua*. *Condor* 85: 503–504.

Adams, N.J., and Klages, N.T. 1989. Temporal variation in the diet of gentoo penguins, *Pygoscelis papua*, at subantarctic Marion Island. *Colonial Waterbirds* 12 (1): 30–36.

Adams, N.J., and Wilson, M.P. 1987. Foraging parameters of gentoo penguins, *Pygoscelis papua*, at Marion Island. *Polar Biol.* 7: 51–56.

Bost, C.A., and Jouventin, P. 1990. Laying asynchrony in gentoo penguins on Crozet Islands: causes and consequences. *Ornis Scandinavia* 21: 63–70.

Bost, C.A., and Jouventin, P. 1991. Evolutionary ecology of gentoo penguins, *Pygoscelis papua*. In *Penguin Biology*, ed. by Lloyd S. Davis and John T. Darby, Academic Press, 85–112.

Bost, C.A., and Jouventin, P. 1991. The breeding performance of the gentoo penguins, *Pygoscelis papua*, at the northern edge of range. *Ibis* 133: 14–25.

Bost, C.A., and Clobert, J. 1992. Gentoo penguins, *Pygoscelis papua*: factors affecting the process of laying a replacement clutch. *Acta Ecologica* 13 (5): 593–605.

Croxall, J.P., and Davis, R.W. 1991. Metabolic rate and foraging behavior of *Pygoscelis* and *Eudyptes* penguins. In *Penguin Biology*, ed. by Lloyd S. Davis and John T. Darby, Academic Press, 207–228.

Davis, R.W., Croxall, J.P., and O'Connell, M.J. 1989. The reproductive energetics of gentoo (*Pygoscelis papua*) and macaroni (*Eudyptes chrysolophus*) penguins at South Georgia. *Journal of Animal Ecology* 58: 59–74.

Haftorn, S., Somme, L., and Gray, J.S. 1981. A census of penguins and seals on Bouvetoya. In *Bouvetoya, South Atlantic Ocean: results from the Norwegian Antarctic research expeditions 1976–77 and 1978–79. Skrieter* 175: Oslo NPI: 29–35.

Trivelpiece, W.Z., and Trivelpiece ,S.G. 1991. Courtship period of Adélie, gentoo, and chinstrap penguins. In *Penguin Biology*, ed. by Lloyd S. Davis and John T. Darby, Academic Press, 113–127.

Trivelpiece, W.Z., Bengtson, J.L., Trivelpiece, S.G., and Volkman, N.J. 1986. Foraging behavior of gentoo and chinstrap penguins as determined by new radiotelemetry techniques. *The Auk* 103: 777–781.

Williams, T.D. 1990. Annual variation in breeding biology of gentoo penguins, *Pygoscelis papua*, at Bird Island, South Georgia. *J. Zool.* (London) 222: 247–258.

Williams, T.D. 1990. Foraging ecology and diet of gentoo penguins, *Pygoscelis papua*, at South Georgia during winter and an assessment of their winter prey consumption. *Ibis* 133: 3–13.

Williams, T.D., and Croxall, J.P. 1990. Is chick fledging weight index of food availability in seabird populations? *Oikos* 53: 414–416.
Williams, T.D., and Croxall, J.P. 1991. Chick growth and survival in gentoo penguins, *Pygoscelis papua*: effect
of hatching asynchrony and variation in food supply. *Polar Biol.* 11: 197–202.
Williams, T.D., Briggs, D.R., Croxall, J.P., Naito, Y., and Kato, A. 1992. Diving pattern and performance in
relation to foraging ecology in the gentoo penguin, *Pygoscelis papua*. *J. Zool.* (London) 227: 211–230.
Williams, T.D., Kato, A., Croxall, J.P., Naito, Y., Briggs, D.R., Rodwell, S., and Barton, T.R. 1992. Diving pat-
tern and performance in nonbreeding gentoo penguins, *Pygoscelis papua*, during winter. *The Auk* 109 (2):
223–234.
Williams, T.D., and Rothery, P. 1990. Factors affecting variation in foraging and activity patterns of gentoo
penguins, *Pygoscelis papua*, during breeding season at Bird Island, South Georgia. *Journal of Applied
Ecology* 27: 1042–1054.
Wilson, R.P. 1989. Diving depths of gentoo, *Pygoscelis papua*, and Adélie, *P. adeliae*, at Esperanza Bay,
Antarctic Peninsula. *Cormorant* 17: 1–8.
Wilson, R.P., Culik, B.M., Adelung, D., Corian, N.R., and Spairani, H.J. 1991. Depth utilization by penguins
and gentoo penguin dive patterns. *J. Orn.* 132: 47–60.

Chinstrap Penguin: *Pygoscelis antarctica*

Haftorn, S. 1986. A quantitative analysis of the behavior of the chinstrap penguin, *Pygoscelis antarctica*, and
macaroni penguin, *Eudyptes chrysolophus*, on Bouvetoya during the late incubation and early nesting
periods. *Polar Research* 4: 33–45.
Haftorn, S., Somme, L., and Gray, J.S. 1981. A census of penguins and seals on Bouvetoya. In *Bouvetoya,
South Atlantic Ocean: results from the Norwegian Antarctic research expeditions 1976–77 and 1978–79*.
Skrieter 175: Oslo NPI: 29–35.
Jazdzewski, K. 1981. Amphipod crustaceans in the diet of *Pygoscelid* penguins of the King George Island,
South Shetland Islands, Antarctica. *Pol. Polar Res.* 2, 3–4: 133–134.
Lishman, G.S. 1985. The comparative breeding biology of Adélie and chinstrap penguins, *Pygoscelis adeliae*
and *P. antarctica*, at Signy Island, South Orkney Islands. *J. Zool.* (London) 205: 245–263.
Lishman, G.S. 1985. The food and feeding ecology of Adélie penguins, *Pygoscelis adeliae*, and chinstrap pen-
guins, *P. antarctica*, at Signy Island, South Orkney Islands. *J. Zool.* (London) 205: 245–263.
Trivelpiece, W.Z., and Trivelpiece, S.G. 1991. Courtship period of Adélie, gentoo, and chinstrap penguins. In
Penguin Biology, ed. by Lloyd S. Davis and John T. Darby, Academic Press, 113–127.
Volkman, N.J., Presler, P., and Trivelpiece, W. 1980. Diets of *Pygoscelid* penguins at King George Island,
Antarctica. *Condor* 82: 373–378.
Wilson, R.P., and Wilson, M-P.T.J. 1989 Tape: a package-attachment technique for penguins. *Wildl. Soc. Bull.*
17: 77–79.

Galapagos Penguin: *Spheniscus mendiculus*

Boersma, D.P. 1975. Adaptations of Galapagos penguins for life in two different environments. In *Biology of
Penguins*, ed. by B. Stonehouse: 101–114.
Boersma, D.P. 1977. An ecological and behavioral study of Galapagos penguins. The living bird. *Cornell
Laboratory of Ornithology*: 43–92.
Boersma, D.P. 1978. Breeding patterns of Galapagos penguins as an indicator of oceanographic conditions.
Science 200, n. 4349: 1481–1483.
Boersma, D.P. 1987. El Ni±o behind penguin deaths? *Nature* 327: 96.
Thouvenaghel, G.T. 1978. Oceanographic conditions in the Galapagos Archipelago and their relationships with
life on the islands. In *Upwelling Ecosystem*, ed. by R. Boje and M. Tomczak, Springer Verlag, 179–200.
Valle, C.A., and Coulter, M.C. 1989. Present status of the flightless cormorant, Galapagos penguin, and greater
flamingo populations in the Galapagos Islands, Ecuador, after the 1982–1983 El Ni±o. *The Condor* 89:
276–281.

Humboldt Penguin: *Spheniscus humboldti*

Bowmaker, J.K., and Martin, G.R. 1985. Visual pigments and oil droplets in the humboldt penguin, *Spheniscus
humboldti. J. Comp. Physiol.* A: 71–77.
Butler, P.J., and Woakes, A.J. 1984. Heart rate and aerobic metabolism in humboldt penguins, *Spheniscus hum-
boldti*, during voluntary dives. *J. Exp. Biol.* 108: 419–428.
Dufy, D.C. 1983. The foraging ecology of Peruvian seabirds. *The Auk* 100: 800–810.
Hays, C. 1984. The humboldt penguin in Peru. *Oryx* 18 (2): 92–95
Hui, C.A. 1985. Maneuverability of the humboldt penguin, *Spheniscus humboldti*, during swimming. *Can. J.
Zool.* 63: 2165–2167.
Johnson, A.W. 1965. *The birds of Chile and adjacent regions of Argentina, Bolivia, and Peru*. Plat
Establicimentos Grafisco, Buenos Aires.
Wilson, R.P., Wilson, M-P., Duffy, D.C., Araya, B., and Klages, N. 1989. Diving behavior and prey of the
humboldt penguin, *Spheniscus humboldti. J. Orn.* 130: 75–79.

Magellanic Penguin: *Spheniscus magellanicus*

Boswall, J., and MacIver, D. 1975. The magellanic penguin, *Spheniscus magellanicus*. In *Biology of Penguins,* ed. by B. Stonehouse: 271–305.

Boersma, P., Stokes, D.L., and Yorio, P.M. 1990. Reproductive variability and historical change of magellanic penguins, *Spheniscus magellanicu,* at Punta Tombo, Argentina. In *Penguin Biology,* ed. by L.S. Davis and J.T. Darby, Academic Press, 13–42.

Scolaro, J.A., and Badano, L.A. 1986. Diet of the magellanic penguin, *Spheniscus magellanicus,* during the chick-rearing period at Punta Claras, Argentina. *Cormorant* 13: 91.

Scolaro, J.A., and Suburo, A.M. 1991. Maximum diving depths of the magellanic penguin. *J. Field Ornithol.* 62 (2): 204–210.

Tompson, K. 1989. *An assessment of the potential for competition between seabirds and fisheries in the F.I.* Falkland Islands Foundation Project.

Woods, R.W. 1970. The avian ecology of a tussock island in the Falkland Islands. *Ibis* 112: 15–24.

Cape Penguin: *Spheniscus demersus*

Cooper, J. 1974. The predators of the jackass penguin, *Spheniscus demersus*. *Bull. B.O.C.* 94 (1): 21–24.

Cooper, J. 1978. Energetic requirement for growth and maintenance of the Cape gannet *(Aves: Sulidae)*. *Zoologica Africana* 13 (2): 305–317.

Heath, R.G.M., and Randall, R.M. 1985. Growth of jackass penguin, *Spheniscus demersus,* on different diets. *J. Zool.* (London) 205 A: 91–105.

Kearton, C. 1941. *L'Ile des manchots*. Boivin and Cie.

Loutit, R., and Boyer, D. 1986. Mainland breeding by jackass penguins, *Spheniscus demersus*. *Cormorant* 13: 27–30.

Rand, R.W. 1960. The biology of guano-producing seabirds: the distribution, abundance, and feeding habits of the cape penguin, *S. demersus,* of the southwestern coast of Cape Province. *Invest. Rep. Div. Fish S. Afr.* 41: 1–28.

Randall, R.M., and Randall, B.M. 1990. Cetaceans as predators of jackass penguins, *Spheniscus demersus*: deductions based on behavior. *Marine Ornithology* 18 (12): 9–12.

Seddon, P.J., and Van Heezik, Y. 1980. Patterns of relief during incubation by jackass penguin, *Spheniscus demersus*. *Proc. IV Pan-Afr. Orn. Congr.*: 227–231.

Seddon, P.J., and Van Heezik, Y. 1991. Hatching asynchrony and brood reduction in the jackass penguin: an experimental study. *Anim. Behav.* 42: 347–356.

Seddon, P.J., and Van Heezik, Y. 1993. Parent offspring recognition in the jackass penguin. *J. Field Ornithol.* 64 (1): 27–31.

Seddon, P.J., and Van Heezik, Y. 1993. Chick creching and intraspecific aggression in jackass penguins. *J. Field Ornithol.* 64 (1): 90–95.

Sivak, J.G. 1976. The role of the flat cornea in the amphibious behavior of the blackfoot penguin, *Spheniscus demersus*. *Can. J. Zool.* 54: 1341–1345.

Sivak, J.G., and Millodot, M. 1977. Optical performance of the penguin eye in air and water. *J. Comp. Physiol.* 119: 241–247.

Van Heezik, Y., and Seddon, P.J. 1990. Effect of human disturbance on beach groups of jackass penguins. *S. Afr. J. Wildl. Res.* 20 (3): 89–93.

Van Heezik, Y., and Seddon, P.J. 1991. Influence of hatching order and brood size on growth in jackass penguins. *S. Afr. J. Zool.* 26 (4): 199–203.

Wilson, R.P., and Wilson, M-P.T. 1989. A peck activity record for birds fitted with devices. *J. Field Ornithol.* 60 (1): 104–108.

Wilson, R.P., and Wilson, M-P.T. 1989. Sharing food in the stomachs of seabirds between adults and chicks. A case for delayed gastric emptying. *Comp. Biochem. Physiol.* 94A, n.3: 461–466.

Wilson, R.P., and Wilson, M-P.T. 1989. Substitute burrows for penguins on guano-free islands. *Le Gerfaut* 79: 125–131.

Wilson, R.P., Wilson, M-P.T., Link, H., Mempel, H., and Adams, N.J. 1991. Determination of movements of African penguins, *Spheniscus demersus,* using system: dead reckoning may be alternative to telemetry. *J. Exp. Biol.* 157: 557–564.

Little Penguin: *Eudyptula minor*

Dann, P. 1992. Distribution, population trends, and factors influencing the population size of little penguins, *Eudyptula minor,* on Philip Island, Victoria. *EMU* 91: 263–272.

Dann, P., and Cullen, J.M. 1990. Survival, patterns of reproductive and lifetime reproductive output of little blue penguins, *Eudyptula minor*. In *Penguin Biology,* ed. by L.S. Davis and J.T. Darby, Academic Press, 63–83.

Cullen, J.M., Montague, T.L., and Hull, C. 1992. Food of little penguins, *Eudyptula minor,* in Victoria: comparison of three localities between 1985 and 1988. *EMU* 91: 318–341.

Stahel, C., and Gales, R. 1987. *Little Penguin: Fairy Penguins in Australia New South Wales*. University Press, 110.

151

Bibliography

Van Heezik, Y. 1990. Diets of yellow-eyed, Fiordland crested, and little blue penguins, breeding sympatrically on Codfish Island, New Zealand. *N.Z.J. Zool.* 17: 543–548.

Waas, J.R. 1988. Acoustic displays facilitate courtship in little blue penguins, *Eudyptula minor. Anim. Behav.* 36: 366–371.

Waas, J.R. 1990. An analysis of communication during aggressive interactions of little blue penguins, *Eudyptula minor.* In *Penguin Biology, e*d. by L.S. Davis and J.T. Darby, Academic Press, 345–373.

Waas, J.R. 1990. Intraspecific variation in social repertoires: evidence from cave- and burrow-dwelling little blue penguins. *Behavior* 115: 63–99.

Waas, J.R. 1991. Do little blue penguins signal their intentions during aggressive interaction with strangers? *Anim. Behav.* 41: 375–382.

Waas, J.R. 1991. The risks and benefits of signaling aggressive motivation: a study of cave-dwelling acoustic little blue penguins. *Behav. Ecol. Sociobiol.* 29: 139–146.

Weavers, B.W. 1992. Seasonal foraging ranges and travels at sea of little penguins, *Eudyptula minor,* determined by radiotracking. *EMU* 91: 302–317.

General Bibliography

Adams, N.J., and Brown, C.R. 1989. Dietary differentiation and trophic relationship in the subantarctic penguin community at Marion Island. *Mar. Ecol. Prog. Ser.* 57: 249–258.

Ausilio, E., and Zotier, R. 1989. Vagrant birds at Kerguelen Island, southern Indian Ocean. *Cormorant* 17: 9–18.

Avery, G. 1985. Late Holocene use of penguin skins: evidence from coastal shell midden at Steenbras Bay, Luderitz Peninsula, South West Africa, Namibia. *Ann. S. Afr. Mus.* 96 (3): 53–65.

Baker, A. de C., Boden, B.P., and Brinton, E. 1990. A practical guide to the *Euphausiids* of the world. Natural History Museum Publication.

Borchgrevink, C.E. 1901. *First on the Antarctic Continent.* George Newnes.

Botswall, J. 1972. The South American sea lion, *Otaria byronia,* as a predator of penguins. *Bull. Brit. Ornith. Club* 92: 129–131.

Busch, B.C. 1985. *The War against the Seals.* McGill-Queens University Press.

Byrd, J. 1946. The Alakaluf. In *Handbook of South American Indians,* 1: *The Marginal Tribes. Bureau of American Ethnology Bull.* 43: 55–79.

Croxall, J.P., and Kirkwood, E.D. 1979. *The Distribution of Penguins on the Antarctic Peninsula and Islands of the Scotia Sea.* B.A.S., Cambridge.

Croxall, J.P., and Lishman, G.S. 1987. The food and feeding ecology of penguins. In *Seabirds' Feeding Ecology and Role in Marine Ecosystems,* ed. by J. Croxall, 101–131.

Davidson, J. 1984. *The Prehistory of New Zealand,* P. Longman.

Fordyce, R.E., Jones, C.M., and Field, B.D. 1986. The world's oldest penguin? *Geol. Soc. N. Z. Newsl.* 74: 56–57.

Fordyce, R.E., and Jones, C.M. 1987. New fossil penguin material from New Zealand. *Abstract. Geol. Soc. N. Z. Misc. Publ.,* n. 37.

Fordyce, R.E., and Jones, C.M. 1990. Penguin history and new fossil material from New Zealand. In *Penguin Biology,* ed. by L.S. Davis and J.T. Darby, Academic Press, 419–446.

Gon, O., and Heemstra, P.C., eds. 1990. *Fishes of the Southern Ocean.* JLB Smith Institute of Ichthyology, Grahamstown, 462.

Hamilton, J.E. 1939. The leopard seal, *Hydrurga leptonyx* (de Blainville). *Discovery Reports* 18: 239–261.

Headland, R.K. 1984. *The Island of South Georgia.* Cambridge University Press.

Hill, H.J. 1990. A new method for the measurement of Antarctic krill, *Euphausia superba. Polar Biol.* 10: 317–320.

Hofman, R.J., Muller-Schwarze, D., Reiche, R.A., and Siniff, D.B. 1977. The leopard seal, *Hydrurga leptonyx,* at Palmer Station, Antarctica. In *Adaptations within Antarctic Ecosystems,* ed. by G.A. Llano, 769–782. *Preceedings of the third SCAR symposium on Antarctic biology,* Aug. 26–30, 1974. Washington, D.C.: Smithsonian Institution.

Hui, C.A. 1988. Penguin swimming I. Hydrodynamics. *Physiol. Zool.* 6 (14): 333–343.

Hui, C.A. 1988. Penguin swimming II. Energetics and behavior. *Physiol. Zool.* 6 (14): 344–350.

Jouventin, P., and Weimerskirch, H. 1990. Long-term changes in seabird populations in the southern ocean. In *Antarctic Ecosystems, Ecological Change and Conservation,* ed. by K.R. Kerry and G. Hempel, Springer Verlag.

Kooyman, G.L. 1981. Leopard seal, *Hydrurga leptonyx,* Blainville, 1820. In *Handbook of Marine Mammals,* 2, ed. by S.H. Ridgway and R.J. Harrison, London Academic Press, 261–274.

Kooyman, G.L., and Davis, R.W. 1987. Diving behavior and performance with special reference to penguins. In *Seabirds' Feeding Ecology and Role in Marine Ecosystems,* ed. by J. Croxall, 63–75.

Kooymann, G., Gentry, R.L., Bergman, W.P., and Hammel, H.T. 1976. Heat loss in penguins during immersion and compression. *Comp. Biochem. Physiol.* 54: 75–80.

Lipps, J.H. 1980. Hunters among the ice floes. *Oceans* 13 (3): 45–47.

Lyndall, R. 1987. *The Aboriginal Tasmanians.* Queensland University Press.

Macadam, J.H., and Walton, D.W.H. 1990. *Ecology and Agronomy of Tussock Grass.* Queen's University of Belfast and British Antarctic Survey, Cambridge.

Marchant, S., and Higgins, P.J. 1990. *Handbook of Australian, New Zealand and Antarctic Birds*, 1, part A, Oxford University Press, Melbourne.

Marion, R., and Sylvestre, J.P. 1993. *Guide des Otaries, Phoques et Siréniens*. Delachaux and Niestlé.

Moss, S. 1988. *Natural History of the Antarctic Peninsula*. Columbia University Press.

Muller-Schwarze, D. 1984. *The Behavior of Penguins*. State University of New York Press.

Munch, P.A. 1945. *Sociology of Tristan Da Cunha*. Results of the Norwegian Scientific Expedition to Tristan Da Cunha 1937–1938, n. 13. Det Norske Videnskap-Akademi, Oslo.

Murphy, R.C. 1927. The Peruvian Guano Islands seventy years ago. *Natural History* 27 (5): 439–447.

Murphy, R.C., and Murphy, G.B. 1959. Peru profits from sea fowl. *Nat. Geo. Mag.* 55 (3): 395–413.

Neris, K.N. 1987. *Cephalopods of the World*. Lourdes and Burges.

Parmelee, D.F. 1980. *Bird Island in Antarctic Water*. University of Minnesota Press.

Parmelee, D.F. 1992. *Antarctic Birds*. University of Minnesota Press.

Penney, R.L., and Lowry, G. 1967. Leopard seal predation on Adélie penguin. *Ecology* 48: 878–882.

Phillips, W.J. 1966. *Maori Life and Customs*, ed. by A.H., and A.W. Reed.

Ponganis, P.J., and Kooyman, G.L. 1990. Diving physiology of penguins. In *Acta XX Congressus Internationalis Ornithologici*, 1887–1892.

Prince, P.A., and Poncet, S. *The Birds of South Georgia*, in press.

Poncet, S., and Poncet, J. 1985. A survey of penguin populations in the South Orkney Islands. *Br. Antarc. Surv. Bull.* 68: 71–81.

Poncet, S., and Poncet, J. 1987. Censuses of penguin populations of the Antarctic Peninsula, 1983–1987. *Br. Antarc. Surv. Bull.* 77: 109–129.

Richardson, J., and Gray, J.E. 1875. *The Zoology of the Voyage of HMS Erebus and Terror 1839–1843*. Janson, London.

Ridoux, V. 1988. Subantarctic krill, *Euphausia vallentini*, preyed upon by penguins around Crozet Islands (southern Indian Ocean): population structure and annual cycle. *Journal of Plankton Research* 10 (4): 675–690.

Ridoux, V. 1993. The diets and dietary segregation of seabirds at the subantarctic Crozet Islands. *Marine Ornithology* 20.

Simpson, G.G. 1971. A review of the pre-Pliocene penguins of New Zealand. *Bull. Am. Mus. Nat. His.* 144: 321–378.

Simpson, G.G. 1976. Notes of variations in penguins and fossil penguins from the Pliocene of Langgebaanweg, Cape Province, South Africa. *Ann. S. Afr. Mus.* 69: 59–72.

Simpson, G.G. 1979. A new genus of late tertiary penguin from Langgebaanweg, South Africa. *Ann. S. Afr. Mus.* 78: 1–9.

Simpson, G.G. 1979. Tertiary penguin from Duinefontein site, Cape Province, South Africa. *Ann. S. Afr. Mus.* 79: 1–7.

Siniff, D.B., and Bengtson, J.L. 1977. Observations and hypotheses concerning the interactions among crab-eater seals, leopard seals, and killer whales. *J. Mamm.* 58 (3): 414–416.

Sparks, J., and Sopper, T. 1987. *Penguins*. David and Charles Publ.

Spellerberg, I.F. 1975. Predators. In *Biology of Penguins*, ed. by B. Stonehouse.

Strange, I. 1983. *The Falkland Island*. David and Charles.

Strange, I. 1992. *A Field Guide of the Falkland Islands and South Georgia*. Harper Collins.

Tollu, B. 1988. *Les Manchots*. Le Rocher.

Tuck, G., and Heinzel, H. 1978. *A Field Guide to the Seabirds of Britain and the World*. Collins.

Watson, G.E. 1975. *Birds of the Antarctic and Subantarctic*. Agu.

Wilson, E. 1980. *Birds of the Antarctic*. New Orchard.

Wilson, E. 1972. *Diary of the Terra Nova Expedition to the Antarctic 1910–1912*. Blandford Press.

Woehler, E.J. 1993. *The Distribution and Abundance of Antarctic and Subantarctic Penguins*. SCAR, Cambridge.

Woods, R.W. 1968. The Avian Ecology of a Tussock Island in the Falkland Islands. *Ibis* 112: 15–24.

Woods, R.W. 1988. *Guide to Birds of the Falkland Islands*, ed. by Anthony Nelson.

Pollution

Barinaga, M., and Lindley, D. 1989. Wrecked ship causes damage to Antarctic ecosystem. *Nature* 337: 495.

Burger, A. E. 1993. Estimating the mortality of seabirds following oil spills: effects of spill. *Marine Pollution Bulletin* 26, 3: 140–143.

Clark, R.B. 1992. *Marine Pollution*, Clarendon Press.

Culik, B.M., Wilson, R.P., Woakes, A.T., and Sanudo, F.W. 1991. Oil pollution of Antarctic penguins: effects on energy metabolism and physiology. *Marine Pollution Bulletin* 22, 8: 388–391.

Eppley, Z.E., and Rubega, M.A. 1989. Indirect effects of an oil spill. *Nature* 340: 510.

Esteves, J.L., and Gracela, Commendatore M. 1993. Total aromatic hydrocarbons in water and sediments in a coastal zone of Patagonia, Argentina. *Marine Pollution Bulletin* 26, 6: 341–342.

Holmes, M. 1973. Oil and penguins don't mix. *Nat. Geo. Mag.* 143, n. 3: 384–395.

Kerley, G.I.H., Erasmus, T., and Mason, R.P. 1985. Effect of molt on crude-oil load in a jackass penguin, *Spheniscus demersus*. *Marine Pollution Bulletin* 16, 12: 474–476.

Bibliography

Moldan, A.G.S., Jackson, L.F., Mc Gibbon, S., and Van Der Westhuizen, J. 1985. Some aspects of the Castillo de Bellver oil spill. *Marine Pollution Bulletin* 16, 3: 97–102.

Monod, J-L., Arnaud, P., and Arnoux, A. 1992. The level of pollution of Kerguelen biota by organochloride compounds during the seventies. *Marine Pollution Bulletin* 24, 12: 626–629.

Muirhead, S.J., and Furness, R.W. 1988. Heavy metal concentrations in the tissues of seabirds from Gough Island, South Atlantic Ocean. *Marine Pollution Bulletin* 19, 6: 278–283.

Randall, R.M., Randall, B.M., and Bevan, J. 1980. Oil pollution and penguins-is cleaning justified? *Marine Pollution Bulletin* 11: 234–237.

Acknowledgments

I especially wish to thank Sally Poncet and Michel Cossec for taking the time to read over the manuscript and for their good advice.

I would also like to thank those people who permitted me to obtain the necessary documentation for this book:

South Africa: J. Cooper (Percy Fitzpatrick Institute), N.J. Adams and M-P. T. Wilson (University of Cape Town)

Falkland Islands: K. Thompson (Falkland Conservation), J. Smith (Museum of Port Stanley)

France: B. Lequette, C. Lefebvre (Museum of Natural History), C.A. Bost (CNRS, CEPE), V. Ridoux (Océanopolis), M-T. Clément (TAAF), Bernard Loyer (Cap Nature), Eric Queinnec (Laboratories of Marine Zoology)

Belgium: J.-M. Dumont

Germany: B. Culik (University of Kiel), R. Wilson

Great Britain: G. Lishman (BAS), J.P. Croxall (BAS)

United States: P. De Boersma (University of Washington), W., and S. Trivelpiece

Norway: S. Haftorn (University of Trondheim)

New Zealand: R.E. Fordyce, P.J. Sedon, and Y.M. Van Heezik (University of Otago), J. Waas

Research for diagrams: Rémy Marion

Photo Credits

Cossec M.: 71
Hadden D.: 94–95
Grunewald O.: 23, 45, 46
Lequette B.: 30–31, 42–43, 113
Marion C., and R.: 8, 10, 11, 15a, 15b, 26, 27a, 27b, 28–29, 33, 35, 36, 51, 53, 54–55, 57, 59, 68–69, 73, 74–75, 77, 78–79, 81, 83, 84–85, 96–97, 99, 100–101, 101, 102, 118–119, 122, 123, 133, 144–145
Monteath C. (Hedgehog House, New Zealand): 62–63
Perreau M.: 82
Rowell G. (Mountain Light): 4–5, 146
Sadoul N.: 39, 127
Sagar P.M., and J.L.: 66–67
Seitre R.: 34, 90–91, 107
Tui De Roy (Hedgehog House, New Zealand): 18–19, 109, 111
Westerkov K. (Hedgehog House, New Zealand): 49, 86
de Wildemberg A.: 105

Index

Index